Winter Light

Sifiso Mpongose was born on 8th August 1979. He lives in Daveyton (Ekurhuleni) the east part of Gauteng, South Africa.

Sifiso is a self starter and a BA Communication Science graduate who has to step up to a father role and responsibilities as well as having to take care of his unemployed mother and four siblings at the tender age of nineteen.

Sifiso enjoyed writing at an early age and has had a way with words ever since he was able to write – his love for words, pen and paper made it easier to express himself in writing rather than speaking.

After he was found permanently unfit to fly as a flight attendant and was grounded for almost two years, he found himself ignited with a passion to pursue and further his studies in order to acquire skills and knowledge to become the best writer and author.

Sifiso Mpongose

Winter Light

Olympia Publishers
London

www.olympiapublishers.com
OLYMPIA PAPERBACK EDITION

A CIP catalogue record for this title is
available from the British Library.

ISBN: 978-1-84897-442-5

(Olympia Publishers is part of Ashwell Publishing Ltd)

First Published in 2014

Olympia Publishers
60 Cannon Street
London
EC4N 6NP

Printed in Great Britain

*This book 'Winter Light' is dedicated to the one I love my God who blessed
me with the gift, talent and a purpose. This one is for you God. To my mother
Busisiwe Patricia Mpongose a.k.a Ndo, to my alter ego and sister Nomsesana
Princess Mpongose a.k.a Sesana. Thank you for all the love and support that
you have given me and I am grateful to have you in my life.*

Acknowledgements

To all the inspiring authors whose books, audio books and DVDs have made a tremendous impact in my life: James Redfield (the Celestine prophecy), Gary Zukav (the seat of the soul), Vincent Peale (the power of positive thinking), E. Lynn Harris (invisible life), Sydney Poitier (the measure of a man), Maya Angelou (I know why the cage bird sings), Robin Sharma (the monk who sold his ferrari), Robin Mack (happiness from the inside out), Rhonda Byrne (the secret), Jack Canfield and Mark Victor Hansen (chicken soup for the soul), Oprah Winfrey shows and 20th DVD anniversary collection. Also, audio books by Joel Osteen (your time), Dr Phil McGraw (real life), Mike Dooley (more notes from the universe) and Michael Bernard Beckwith (spiritual liberation).

All these books, audio books and DVDs I have read, listened and watched. They ignited my passion to write my own book and gave me hope, love, and life.

Lastly to my blunt and frank best friend who was with me during my trial time, giving me advice and sharing his precious time with me; Derek Boze Namane Moeketsi.

The rape child… Perseverance

Perseverance, the rape child…

What's in the name, you give to your child? For their future

What's in the name that your family gives you? Question.

My name is Perseverance. Why?

My name speaks volumes

Why name Perseverance…question?

Who gives a child such a name?

The mother of success that I am

Eat your heart out… P.S my initials, take note

HOW POWERFUL IS MY NAME?

I used to hate my English name

The meaning of my English name

Thank you, for giving me the name… Perseverance

I love the name Perseverance

I hate the name Perseverance

I am not perseverance

My name's a wish, a dream that's Sifiso

Mpongose or Jinika or double barrel? Question

Mpongose- Jinika, who gives a continental? I don't

Who cares? I found God in me and I love him fiercely

The new credo of P S Mpongose

My new credo

My mantra these days

You are not alone my friend

Let us dance in the rain

When it rains, it pours

Be still and silent

Finding my higher self

Investing in yourself first

My winter light

Pain the pivotal teacher

My character expansion

My character development

Preparation leads to luck

Introduction/ Preface

For too long I was unhappy. I grew up painfully shy and in my high school days I was actually a loner and found it hard to make friends. I could not fit in with the boys my age but I got along with girls mostly. Those days I was closer with my cousin sisters and we had a tight relationship. I felt totally left out when I was in the company of boys because they would discuss soccer and their girlfriends.

Those days I tried so hard but I felt so awkward and uncomfortable with my peers. I was an introvert, which I think I still am and I wonder sometimes why that is, because most of the Leos' I know are out there are extroverts. Anyway I was teased quite a lot in my primary and high school days. Kids can be vicious sometimes. Those days for me were tough and sometimes painful.

My mother was a disciplinarian and caregiver who raised and supported five children with no permanent job. She had a lot of pain and used to beat me like crazy. However I grew up to be such a responsible man despite all the struggles and challenges. She lovingly guided and cared for us in ways some children never knew.

Despite my loving family I found myself consistently unhappy in many ways. Even at a young age life seemed like a lot of hard work for little or no reward and hardly any lasting satisfaction at all. I contemplated suicide once in my life. I was miserable and angry because I had so many dreams about my life. I just decided one day to write a suicide letter. Come to think of it now, God knows that was just my way of getting attention because I felt that time that no one was hearing me or understanding my pain. I felt useless as a human being and all I wanted was to do something about my life to be given a chance to prove myself and help my mother and siblings to get a better life.

I was the breadwinner at home and it was financially stressful to support five people on one salary but I did it and I do not know how; I did all that by the grace and power of God (I believe I just answered my own question). When it comes to suicide I do not think I had the courage to kill myself to be quite honest, but I was depressed I can tell you that. Since I did not have the guts to end my life, my other option was to fix it. I had to go out there and do it and stop thinking that being miserable was fashionable. I have learned a lot in my short life. As I am getting old I am actually in a journey to happiness. It's a learning process but I have come a long way. I use what works for me and lose what does not. I always wanted to change my circumstances in order to become happier. This was my major focus in my life, I thought if I could be successful and change these circumstances like seeking greater wealth, status and educational attainment, it would make me happier but it did not bring me or lead me to any lasting happiness. The only thing I got from changing my life circumstances was the temporary high and pleasure and this does not necessary make me lastingly happier. This does not mean though that money did not buy happiness – it can, but only to some extent. Money can buy status, freedom and some degree of control over the circumstances of my work and life. I really thought that success would bring happiness in my life. I was playing the right game by the wrong rules. I played it by the book and never questioned the assumptions by which I lived my life or the rules by which I conducted myself. I just kept on trying harder.

Giving my best never seemed to be good enough. I lived the better part of my life being frustrated and playing by the wrong rules. The truth of the matter is that I have worked hard or had worked hard or I was working hard for too long at the wrong things. I knew that there was something wrong because I was unhappy, in pain and feeling frustrated. I know that I was meant to succeed and be abundantly rich. Something was wrong in my life; it was not the circumstances of my life that were wrong but the consciousness that created those circumstances. I am not my circumstance...

Chapter 1

I am wondering in the winter light. It is Saturday evening. I am alone trying to figure out who I am. Why am I here? Why am I in this situation? And when will I come out of this challenge? I wonder when this season will change? I know that in a year there are four different seasons and I guess as a human being I have to deal with nature and try to prepare myself for each and every season in this earth school. Stars glowing in the twilight tell me true. Hope whispers and I will follow, till you love me too.

How it all started… God had his eyes on me, had designed me for glorious living. I always tell everyone that I know I was not born to be poor and I feel that, almost every time. I am getting closer into living a glorious and abundant life that God has created for me. It is hard to believe this, especially if you are facing hard times, because I ask myself these questions: where is God? At this point, does he love me? I ask myself, why Lord? Why me? I mean, I have been through a lot already – can I please get a break? I tell him that this is so unfair. I have come to a conclusion and stopped asking myself these questions and I say if not me, who else? I thank the Lord although I do not understand sometimes.

My Story

I am the first born child – named Sifiso, meaning a wish come true by my grandmother. My English name is Perseverance and my mother had me when she was only sixteen years old. I was born in a poor family. We were living in a two bedroom house with my great-grandmother, my grandmother, my mother and my four siblings. It was a crowded house, as you can imagine. My family was close and happy, but come weekends there would be lots of fights and bickering, because alcohol was always involved. Gossip, jealousy and envy were always there, as you would expect; this house was crowded and there were a lot of females. I thought one day, if only I could be something and try to make this house bigger for all of us, then maybe everyone would get along. The house was small for all of us and we were always on each other's toes.

Things changed when I reached sixteen, I was doing commerce subjects at high school. By that time I wanted to work for a bank or be a chartered accountant. My forte was accounting, economics and business economics, so I figured I could make it since I was getting good grades. I started to apply for bursaries with auditors. Delloite & Touche was one of my favorite companies and my first option. By the time I was finishing my matriculation I had applied to all the banks. I only got one response at FNB bank and when I went for the interview I thought, this is it, I am going to be a bank teller, wow! I would be just like my father, because I'd heard that my father was working for a bank and to think, I had never even met or seen the man. My mother never wanted to discuss him or tell me more about him; she is always so defensive when I ask her to take me to him. I got a rejection letter a few weeks after my interview with FNB Bank and a bunch of others from all the different companies that I applied to for bursaries. My dream to become one of the few black chartered accountants went down the drain. I was disappointed but in my mind I could see my name written somewhere on paper as Mr P.S. Mpongose (CA).

Nevertheless, less than two years later, after all the anger, frustration and stress – I'd even written a suicide letter, because at that moment I felt I was knocking on closed doors and all I wanted was a chance to prove myself. There was nothing for me in this world. Firstly I wanted to further my education and I was eager to do that, but nobody was there to help me achieve it. Luckily enough I had a chance to meet a whole lot of good people who guided me and helped me to find a job. I did find odd jobs here and there but I did not have a choice at that time.

Eventually I found my dream job. Actually it was more like a lifestyle. It was 18th December 1998 when my dreams came true. I was appointed at one of the prestigious airlines in South Africa; I was now P.S. Mpongose (CA). I was a cabin attendant, not a chartered accountant, and I was happy with that. Every time I printed my roster at work it read CA P.S. Mpongose, (sometimes I would print ten copies at a time) I was ecstatic and I thought, wow! Be careful what you ask for or write in your journal. This was a perfect time for me to get my family out of my great gran's house as I knew my mother was not happy staying with my siblings there. We rented a house that was perfect for a family of six. I could not buy a house at that time until I turned twenty-one. I was only nineteen, so I had to wait two years, and bought the house as soon as I turned twenty-one. My family and I were happy and only to find out later about the house. I had a drawing of it in one of my old accounting school books. I was so amazed at the findings and how precise the drawing was, but it was actually meant for my great gran's house because at that time I just wanted to extend my gran's house so that everyone could have their space and live in harmony.

Now I thought, this is what I was created for in this universe. I was living a glorious life. I was happy that I'd managed to get my mother and my siblings a place called home and now that they could get the respect they deserved in the community. It was a great achievement from my side and I was proud of myself and I am still proud. These are just a few moments in my glorious life.

My journey continues and I am glad that I can count on my family to be there for me every step of the way. As they say, "a journey is always better when it is shared", and I say, be careful who you choose to share your journey with, because if you follow the crowd you end up getting lost in it, so I choose wisely. I am so grateful every day that I have a relationship with God. I ask my God every day to guide me and teach me. I know now that I was created by God for God. I know that he planned me before I existed without any of my input. I am here now, so what is it that I am supposed to do? I get confused sometimes as to how he does his things. I ask the questions, does he love me? Why did he create me and let me suffer in this vicious world? I ask my Lord, do you love me? I think to myself, I did not choose to be here; you chose me and I did not have any input at all. Sometimes I even feel he is not here. I feel he just decided to go on holiday and come to think of it I would understand with everything that is happening around the world. I think he really needs a holiday. This world is crazy and it is just too much for him I guess. I still believe though that he did not create me to suffer or to be poor. One thing is for sure, I will get there, I will live the glorious and abundant life he created for me. Hope and believing in him are my keys to happiness and fulfillment.

I have faith in my Lord and I know that my parents did not plan to have me, because my mother was still a child herself, only sixteen when she brought me into this earth school.

I do not know my father – he just disappeared, and is nowhere to be found. I do not even have a picture of my father not even in my mind. The thought of not knowing him used to sadden me. But now I know he is not worth my anger and my sadness. Previously I tried to contact him in order for us to meet because at that time I had a lot of questions for him and my mother was not willing to answer all of them. What bothered me was the question, do I look like him? I wanted to even do a DNA test to prove if he was my father or not. I was angry, frustrated and needed a father-figure in my life. I was going through my life as a teenager and I really needed him at that point in my life. I am a man now thanks to my mother and I know she is proud of me. I must say it took me sometime to realize that my father wanted nothing to do with me and I forgive him for that with all my heart. Now I know that I was not an accident, God had planned me, I was expected to be here and thank you God for that…

A note to my unknown father: Thank you regardless of the circumstances of my birth, for the right genetic makeup to create the custom-made me that God had in mind. Thank you for your DNA, I know you do not love me and I am okay with that because God made me so that he could give me all the love in the world. God will always take care of me. He has carried me since I was born and will carry me even when I am old, which is something that you, my unknown father, will never and was never able to do.

I must say it was not easy not having a father in my life but I am all grown up and I turned out to be such a responsible man. At this point I do not miss having a father in my life because I did not have a father when I was growing up. All I remember was when I was three years old I visited my so-called father and his wife and their child. Sadly I cannot picture my father's face. I guess I cannot miss what I did not have, and it was a blessing in disguise I think. I really do not think he would have been comfortable with my sexual orientation. Now I know God created me as I am. I am not chance, nor luck, nor coincidence, nor mistake or mishap or accident. God wanted me and created me to be exactly as he wanted, full stop.

Chapter 2

My life has been driven by guilt. I guess it happens to all of us. I spend my entire life running from regrets and hiding their shame. It goes on and on in my mind. I wish I had done it this way or the other way, I wish I had not gone there, I should have trusted my gut, I should have listened and stopped being stubborn.

I get lost sometimes and I envy those people who always say, "I go with my gut feeling." Well let me tell you something. I always get so confused with this gut feeling thing, because when I am in a situation there are so many voices and I do not know which one I should trust. These are some of the regrets that drove my life. I regret not listening to my family when they told me that I was not fit to drive my car. I did not listen and at that time I convinced myself that I could make it safely, that this was my car so if something bad was supposed to happen, it would happen. I was tempting fate and not even thinking about my life or the lives of the people I could endanger. Look at me now. I am without a car, I struggle to get to work, and I pay too much for Maxi Taxi. I ask myself where are all those friends that I was always with, when I had my car? Here I am alone with nobody to help me, when I really need a car to go work. So the question is, should I have listened more, would my car then still be running? Another guilt that was haunting me was that I knocked a child over, and I felt so bad I guess I was manipulated by that memory. I allowed my past to control my future. Every time I drove the car I would always tense up and I always felt as if something very bad was going to happen and guess what? Something bad always happened. I would also hear funny sounds in my car while I was driving; this is why all the accidents happened to me, because I was always ready for something bad to happen. I was unconsciously punishing myself by sabotaging my own success. I was a prisoner of my own guilt; it was eating me up every day to think that I could have killed a child. It was a nightmare and at that time I was even driving without a license. If it was not, "Oh my God, I think this car is going to stop any second from now", it was "Oh my God, I hope I don't get stopped by the traffic cops." Funnily enough, all these things happened. God has cleared my record. I know this because he specializes in giving people a fresh start.

My life was driven by resentment and anger and I thought that if I hold on to my hurt, it will remind me to be extra careful about certain people and situations because I will always refer to it every time. I hate when people say, get over it and move on. I always failed to understand why should I? Since I was a victim, to me the whole idea was to make the other person suffer as well and feel what I went through by hating them. I would always rehearse my pain and anger over and over in my mind, not letting it go for a second. I would tell people, can I just feel my pain? I would drag it with me forever and sometimes I would explode at others – especially my family, and of course most of the time they would have nothing to do with it. I would shut out people that I loved because I felt I needed to nurse my precious pain and I guess I still do that and now, I call it "me time" or, "I need some introspection." Now I have found out that I can release my pain through forgiveness. Resentment always hurts me more than it does the person I resent, so if I hold on to pain, hurt and resentment the offender has the power over me, but if I forgive them I take back my power and carry on with my life. One thing is for sure – those who have hurt me in the past cannot continue to hurt me now unless I hold on to pain through resentment. My past is past! Nothing will change it. I was only hurting myself with my bitterness and I decided to learn from it and then let it go. To worry myself to death with resentment, anger, and hurt was a foolish and senseless thing to do. Now I forgive, learn from it and let it go. I feel lighter when I do that and I am able to carry on living my life.

My life was driven by fear and I ended up missing great opportunities because I was afraid of venturing out of my comfort zone. The main key here is I that am afraid of rejection big time! There are things that I would really like to do, like trying some modeling, but I am afraid of rejection. I always think, who do you think you are, Sifiso? There are a lot of good looking people out there with great physiques and it is a tough competition. I am always wishing someone would just find or spot me somewhere, like one of those modeling or talent scouts, so that I do not have to go to the effort of making my portfolio and finding an agent. I was looking at my face today and I thought, wow! God really took his time in creating my features, damn! If only God gave me talent. I think he gave me my good looks, and I hope someday I will get the courage to use what God has given me, instead of sitting by and waiting for every opportunity to come to me. I play it safe and try to avoid risks. When I try to console myself I say: I have too many responsibilities, but I trust that one day I will banish all my fears and do what I really feel passionate about and be fulfilled.

I am a little driven by "materialism" and I guess there are different levels; I am on level one (I hope and wish). I say this because I know life is not about things and money, although I cannot help wanting a beautiful home with grand appliances and gadgets, having a nice car, beautiful clothes and to be able to live a comfortable and secure life. All I know is that I have to have some kind of balance. Possessions only provide temporary happiness. All I am saying is, yes I would like to have nice things but my value is not determined by my valuables. My relationship with God is the real security that cannot be taken away from me.

I need "approval", but only from God and the people who matter most to me, especially my mother. I do not allow anybody's expectations to control my life. I only do what makes me happy. All I know is that I am a very strong person and I have got a strong personality. I am not worried by what others might think, especially people that I do not know or care about. I must say though, it took me some time to do or say the things that I wanted to. Usually I would follow the crowd and get lost, and I have realized that you cannot make everyone happy. I am myself and I do not try to fit in. I ended up living a lie because I needed to change myself in order to get approval from certain groups of friends or at work. I am so proud that I know myself now and this is me, take it or leave it. I won't try to conform for anybody just because I need their approval. What is surprising is the more I am myself, the more I relax and I do not have to keep up appearances, and guess what? People get to know and love the real me, the real Sifiso. It is a great feeling. Yes, I would like approval from my mother on certain things and decisions, her approval matters to me. Now I know if I need approval, then God is always there. I do not have to be controlled by the opinions of others because I end up not using my full potential, attracting unnecessary stress and living an unfulfilled life. God is driving my life and knowing God gives meaning to my life.

Chapter 3

I am a spiritual person and I believe in God, but I get confused sometimes because I believe in my ancestors, I believe in astrology and psychics. How should I balance everything? I found out recently by going to consult a sangoma because I felt my life had come to a complete standstill. I was drowning in credit card debt I could not pay my debts on time. My second house bond was in arrears, my love life was non-existent. I found out that my ancestors wanted me to slaughter a cow for them and that is why my life came to a standstill. Apparently they were not happy where they were and were holding all my blessings, money, luck and all the things that I thought I deserved.

I was livid when the sangoma told me this because I thought, how could they want a cow while they're holding everything? It was crazy, ridiculous, really! How can I buy a cow when I cannot even buy myself basic food? Surely they expected me to rob a bank or something? Anyway we had to cleanse ourselves, first me and my family and that was money – money I did not have. I thought, let me take my last money that I was supposed to pay my credit cards with and just do it and get it over and done with and see what happens. Well, we did it. We went to Polokwane, they slaughtered a goat and we were covered with a goat's freshly digested food. I believed that once this was done my life would start moving. I started talking with my ancestors, asking them to show me some light so that I would be able to buy the cow they needed. Let me say my life was still at a standstill and I totally forgot about God.

Then I went to New York and for no apparent reason I was drawn to the sign of a psychic, and I decided to just go in and check it out. I expected some shady place with candles and crystals, I expected a dodgy character but I was surprised. The place looked like one of those posh New York apartments. The psychic's name was Bobby, a classy woman. She did not look anything like Whoopi Goldberg in that *Ghost* movie. She told me things I could not believe. She was fumbling at the beginning but after a while she was on point. What I am saying is I know God drives my life and gives meaning to my life but I also believe in my ancestors. I believe that no matter what, they play some role in my life. So the question is – how do I balance the two: do they co-exist? To be honest I do not know, I play it by ear and I go with the flow. With God I can bear anything but at this point my life had no direction, I was on survival mode. I was actually struggling to even survive. Maybe if I slaughtered the cow my life would start moving forward again. All I know is God has good plans for me and he is not planning to hurt me. I have hope; that is why I am able to cope in this current situation, because hope comes from having God in my life and God will give me hope and a good future. Knowing God simplifies my life. I live a plain, simple, full life. I try to do what is important. I allocate and use all my time effectively and use all my resources. I try to do things right the first time. I like to have plenty of time to prepare. I do not do too much, I hate doing things at the last minute because I don't like being pushed. I try to do one thing at a time. I found out that multi-tasking is not for me because when I do that I end up messing everything up.

I have got peace of mind. I focus on what is important, which is God and my family. I became effective by being selective, I focus my energy on one thing at a time, forgetting the past and looking forward to what lies ahead. I get so motivated by just thinking what is going on in my life. God is here with me and he will always be with me no matter what. Sometimes I cannot even feel his presence but faith and hope keeps me motivated. I have learned that I am a powerful person, everything I want eventually happens or I make it happen with help from God. I talk about it, I verbalize my dreams, I write them down, I pray about them and they always occupy my mind. So now I always try to monitor my thoughts, although it a difficult process. I try to hold on to my positive feelings and when I am feeling depressed and down I acknowledge those feelings and that is when I need some time alone with my God or loved ones. Changing negative feelings is not easy but I have my way of getting myself out of those feelings by playing soulful music, reading my spiritual books or just cleaning and sorting my room and my paperwork, bills or even filing. What works most for me is writing all those negative feelings and thoughts in my journal that helps me immensely. It takes away the load; I just give all my baggage to my Lord God and pray that he gives me strength to carry on with my life.

I enjoy variety and maybe that is why I am still doing what I do for a living. It's been years and I am still enjoying it so much. I feel I still have a lot to do before I even think of resigning. I love the flexibility of my working hours. I do not have to work nine to five, I do not have to face traffic every day, I work with different people and every day is an exciting challenge. I get some time out and to reset myself when I go overseas. I love my off days and I always get excited when I do my shopping overseas, getting all the things that I cannot find them here in South Africa. Lastly the meal allowance is the icing on the cake; it helps me achieve even more than a highly educated normal working person with all their degrees. I do things quickly and easily. I love beautiful things and people, I am organized and I know what is important. I try to get things done in time; I prioritize and spend my time effectively. I know that I am wise because I have got a clear purpose and that is the foundation on which I base my decisions, allocate time and use all my resources. I am creative, I love putting things together, I love cooking and fashion, and sometimes I feel I could be a fashion guru. I love decorating my house and playing with ideas and of course I love when a plan comes together. I love writing; give me a pen and paper any time and I can spend all day just writing. There are other more important things that I do though, they make me so excited and when I do them I feel fully alive and I know when I am fully alive I bring glory to God.

I worship my Lord, for me worshiping him means I enjoy his company. I make sure each time I remember just to say thank you for today and I make time for us to spend some intimate quality time and I do this by just writing my thoughts for the day, telling him all my troubles and fears, telling him all I am grateful for, counting my blessings and thanking him for all the things that he has done for me. Worship is the lifestyle of enjoying God, loving him and giving myself to be used for his good purposes. I love others and I try not to judge. I have learned to accept people as they are, because I know that the Lord has accepted me as I am. I try to become like Christ by acknowledging everybody and giving them eye contact when I greet them because a common denominator in human society is that everyone wants to know that you can see them and you can hear them. No matter where you come from or background we all want to be heard and seen. I give help to others with all my strength and energy that God supplies. I serve others, especially my family with all my gifts, talents, skills and abilities without any selfish purposes. I let God's generosity flow through me and sometimes I wonder, how did I do all these wonderful things? I love the feeling it brings to me. I feel so high I can go to heaven and back. The whole idea of giving my services to others brings complete joy and happiness to my soul. Funnily enough when I share my gifts with others I do not expect anything from them, I always tell them to take it, feel it and pass it on. This means, take all my gifts or help or advice or whatever that I am serving you with, feel it and let it help you and when you are okay and sorted, pass it on to somebody who really needs help.

Sometimes I wonder how I really make all these wonderful and good things happen. It is no secret. I tell everyone about God and the universe. I tell everyone about the laws of attraction. I know the truth about God and I am so privileged to have his power and I will try to introduce everyone who is willing to listen. The truth is, I believe that God loves me and he made me for his purpose. I believe I am not an accident. No matter what I have done, God wants to forgive me. The second truth is, I receive Jesus into my life as my Lord and Savior. I receive his forgiveness for all my sin, I receive his spirit, which gives me power to fulfill my life purpose. We all want to hear the truth but let's be honest, the truth hurts, it really hurts, but it is bearable when you have Jesus Christ as your friend.

When I found out that life is a test and every second of the day I am being tested by the devil himself, I was a little bit frustrated with this truth. I wondered why the Lord would allow that to happen to people that he loves. I wanted an easy life full of happiness and joy, an abundant life with no hiccups, but hey, it rarely happens in this world. With every second of my life, every thought, every temptation, every trial and tribulation, this truth is just too much. But guess what, Satan continuously tests people's character, faith, obedience, love, integrity and loyalty. I know that I am always being tested and every time God watches my reaction or response, he watches how I respond to people, problems, success, conflict, illness, disappointment, even the weather. He even watches the simplest action such as how I answer my phone. A very important test is how I act when I cannot feel God's presence in my life. This test happens to me almost every time. I feel he sometimes draws back so that I won't sense his closeness. I know now that with every test that Satan gives me I get stronger and I find out more about myself. Nothing is insignificant in my life; even the smallest incident has significance for my character development. Every day is an important day and every second is a growth opportunity to deepen my character. What bothers me is that some of these opportunities I don't even notice, but all of them have eternal implications. The good news is God never gives me tests I cannot handle. He always gives me the strength to endure it and so provides me with a way out. Another truth that I found was that God gave me my life because he trusted me enough to take care of it and use it for his purpose. I sometimes feel I do not deserve his trust and I feel I disappoint him most of the time. Firstly I do not take care of my body the way I am supposed to. My great concern is my smoking habit, I pray to God for strength every day to help me stop smoking, but I always fail. Every time I tell myself I am going to stop smoking, something bad happens to me that makes me stressed out, and guess what? I go back to smoking, I know this is probably in my mind, but especially when I am stressed, smoking calms me down and I can think straight after I have a few puffs. For me this really works well, but deep down I want to quit because I know in the long run I might develop lung cancer, God forbid. I know every time I smoke I damage my lungs. That is the fact, I try and try to stop but – bang! Something stresses me and guess what? I keep on relapsing, but hey I am going to keep on trying and I hope God will give me strength. God trusted me by giving me my body and here I am smoking my lungs out. I am actually showing him that I am not worthy of that trust. I must make it last forever, take care of myself, my body, I must eat well, exercise and stop smoking. From now on I will take care of my body because God owns it and he trusted me well enough for me to take the best care of it. Life is a test and trust and the more God gives me, the more responsible he expects me to be. Well, I know that I am not going to be here for long but I always thought that since I am here I might as well leave my footprints everywhere I go, leave something that people will talk about, some kind of a mark. I don't want to leave this earth school without anyone noticing, I want to leave with a bang! I want my name to be remembered, I wanted to leave some sort of lasting legacy here on Earth but living to create an earthly legacy is a short-sighted goal. I realize that all achievements are eventually surpassed. I always want to achieve more or do better than the last time. I push myself to the limit; I want to excel in everything I do. I want bigger, better achievements and I failed to realize that again and again records are broken, reputations fade and tributes are forgotten and ultimately what matters most will not be what others say about my life, but what God will say. Now I use my time wisely to build an external legacy and just knowing that God has the last say about how I live my life here on Earth. I am here on Earth for just a little while, my time here is brief; this is not my home. I won't be here for long so I try not to get too attached to worldly possessions and achievements.

I try not to worry about having it all on earth, because the things I see now are here today, gone tomorrow. The things I cannot see now will last forever. This explains why some of God's promises seem unfulfilled, some prayers seem unanswered and some circumstances seem unfair. This is his way of trying to keep me from becoming too attached to Earth. I am not completely happy here and I cannot be truly and completely happy. There is always a hole in my heart that I have to constantly fill and no matter how much I fill the hole, it's always running on empty. I am not supposed to be completely happy here; it's time to prepare myself for something better. I did not know that God has emotions too; maybe that is why they say we were made in his emotion. I wonder if it is true that God may be one of us, maybe he's here on Earth with us living as a human being. Since he has emotions there are ways of bringing pleasure to God; some of these I was doing, not even aware that I was making God happy. Some of them I must try out because I know it is not for my pleasure but for God's enjoyment.

Chapter 4

I connect with God. I talk to him everywhere I am; I write to him whenever I can, it is my lifestyle. I talk about him every chance I get and some people think maybe I am crazy because I go on and on about how spiritual I am and how I have a great intimate relationship with God. I thank him for giving me a chance to try again and giving me air to breathe and strength to face another day.

During my day, if I remember, I try to do little acts of kindness to total strangers and I act Christ-like. I say, this is for you my Lord. I do tasks at work that nobody wants to do because I know that God will be smiling at me and will take notice. I volunteer at every opportunity if my help is needed and I do it with all my energy and afterwards I feel so powerful. I like the way I do things sometimes. I do them Christ-like and I know that my Lord is very joyful wherever he is. He is proud of me and I am glad I fell in love with Jesus Christ.

The next thing I must do is to go to church more often. I do not like to go to church because I do not like people acting "holier than thou", and I do not like the judging. I notice that people forget that they are human as well and they like grouping themselves according to class. That is not supposed to happen in church. I guess I can keep on looking but I will never find a perfect church without its politics. I will from now on go to church every chance I get because I know it is not for my benefit. Worship is not for me, it is for God. I promise myself that I will worship my Lord every second, everywhere I am and whatever I am doing, I will dedicate it to God and perform it with an awareness of his presence. This is for you my Lord, I know that you are smiling right now, enjoy, it is for your pleasure, not mine.

I am so glad that I make God smile in so many ways and I try to live my everyday life by pleasing him every chance I get. I love my God more than anything else in the world. I have a relationship with my Lord and it is very intimate, he loves me and I love him back, he revealed himself to me by creating me, now I know him and I have fallen in love with him and I try to spend as much time as possible with him, so that our relationship will be more closer and tighter. My Lord is my number one and I trust him completely even when it does not make sense. I have no doubt because I have faith that he knows what is best for my life. I obey him wholeheartedly, I try not to complain too much or make excuses. I always expect him to keep his promises, help me with all my problems, and do the impossible when necessary. When all my prayers and dreams are manifested I give praise to him and thank him continually. I appreciate everything that he has done for me, I adore him and I always express my gratitude to him by writing in my journal. I use all my abilities to help others. I am what I am and I don't try to be someone else because God loves me just as I am. God knows that I am incapable of being perfect or sinless and he loves me still.

I thought that surrendering myself to God was a once-off prayer and I would be good to go. There is a difference between the moment of surrender and the practice of surrender. A moment of surrender is what I normally would do by giving the Lord all my troubles, fears, disappointments, anger, jealousy, self-pity and all my baggage. That is when I feel helpless and it hits me. I face the reality that I am not in charge of my life and I surrender to my Lord. I ask him to take away all the pain and show me whatever I am supposed to learn from the problem. God gets my attention with subtle methods, starting with red flags in order for me to learn something, but if I am not paying attention then – BANG! A huge wake-up call and I end up wondering why? It is because I was not paying attention to the little red flags he was giving me. I give myself completely to him, not out of fear or duty, but in love, I know God wants my life and he wants all of it, one hundred percent. I am not in control of my life. He is the driver in my life. I trust him and I know him better now. I admit that I have my limitations. All I do now is my best and I surrender it to my God. I stopped giving orders and interfering with God's work within me. I accepted that I cannot have it all and now I do not get upset when things do not go my way. I surrender to God and I rely on God to work things out instead of me trying to manipulate others, force my agenda and control the situation. I let it go! I let God work because he is always in charge. Instead of trying harder, I wait patiently for him because now I trust him even more. I have peace and freedom when I do that and I feel lighter. Surrendering myself is the only way I live my life. The practice of surrender which I think is the most difficult is moment-by-moment and it is life-long. It is a daily thing. I may have to re-surrender my life fifty times a day. I must make it a habit. I am sure I will be able to follow him, which means I must give up the things I want and my life daily. I totally surrender my life, this decision will be tested. Sometimes it will mean doing inconvenient, unpopular, costly or seemingly impossible tasks. It will often mean doing the opposite of what I feel like doing.

God is my best friend. I have constant conversation with him throughout the day. I try to include him in all of my activities and situations or problems and even every thought. The key to friendship with God, he said, is not changing my attitude toward what I do. I pray all the time by using breath prayer: "I surrender all." Thinking about it I used to do this but in a singing kind of way. I must do it more. I will try meditation. If I know how to worry I already know how to meditate so I must focus on God's word. I honestly share my feelings with God and I trust him when he asks me to do something. I have learned to care about what he cares about. I am completely honest about all my faults and I know he does not expect me to be perfect and I know he knows when I lie to him because he can see everything. I must say I am quite frank with him. I often vent all my anger and frustration to him. I complain, second guess, accuse and argue with him. I question and challenge him because sometimes I feel I have been cheated or disappointed and I blame him for everything that is going wrong in my life. I say it like it is. Now I realize that God always acts in my best interest, even when it is painful and I do not understand it. Realizing my anger and revealing my feelings is the first step to healing and expressing my doubt is sometimes the first step toward the next level of intimacy with God. This time God wants it, all he wants all of me. I will praise my Lord accurately and authentically and I am going to do it my way, because God intentionally made us all different and why should everyone be expected to love God in the same way? God loves variety, there is no "one size fits all" when it comes to loving and worshiping God; God wants me to be myself. I do not worship to be seen by others or to please myself. I deliberately shift the focus off myself. Sometimes it is not convenient or comfortable but I worship him no matter what, even when I do not feel like it.

Sometimes I am exhausted and worn, but when all I want to do is sleep I worship him because I know it pleases him. It is easy to worship God when things are going well in my life. The deepest level of worship is praising God in spite of pain thanking God during a trial, trusting him when tempted, surrendering while suffering and loving him when he seems distant. One thing I will tell you for sure, there was never a time when I would say I felt God's presence. Sometimes I feel all these kinds of emotions and I think to myself there is no way I could be feeling his presence, maybe it is just a mix of emotions and energy or maybe I am so desperate to feel his presence that I am making everything up with my emotions. God is always distant with me when I need him. Sometimes he ignores my cries for help and he is nowhere to be found when I am in a crisis. It feels that when I pray to him my prayers bounce off the ceiling. This is painful and frustrating but I know now it is important for my development and faith. I feel he is angry with me at that moment or maybe he is disciplining me for some sin. I get so livid because I cannot feel his presence and I do not understand why I should keep praising him when he is so silent. Now I know that he wants me to sense his presence, but he is more concerned that I trust him than that I feel him. I used to fall apart asking myself a lot of questions. How do I keep on doing this if God is nowhere to be found? How do I stay connected in this crisis without communication? Where are you, my friend? I thought we were close, can you see me? Can you hear me? At that point my faith is stretched to the limit.

No matter what, come rain or shine I will praise my Lord, I will always stay close to him. I will always remember what God has done for me. I have my life today because of what Jesus did for me on the cross. God's son died for me so that I could have everything. He died so that I could live forever and to think that Jesus could have saved himself but did not because he was not selfish, he trusted God and most of all Jesus wanted to save me. I do not know about you but that alone is worthy of my continual thanks and praise. Never again will I wonder what I have to be thankful for. Thank you Jesus, thank you for saving my life.

Chapter 5

It took a long time for me to accept myself the way God created me. It was a long, painful process coming out to my family. It was a difficult time for me and probably even worse for them. I did not understand why I was so different, why I was feeling that way. I believed it was a sin and I was going to hell.

It was hard growing up and people used to call me names but it was worse when I went to church and I promise you, almost every time I went to church it was always confirmed that my life was a sin and I was going to hell. A normal person like me would choose what they call an alternative lifestyle. I would not dare to choose this alternative lifestyle, it is a tough one. People always call you names, you have to defend yourself all the time, you have to lie. I had to be someone else in order to get people's approval and then they would ask me the marriage question and I had to create lie after lie. I avoided situations where I would be asked those questions, especially in church because I knew that they were disgusted by people like me.

I am at peace with who I am now. I am myself and I accept that fully because I know any time I reject any part of myself, I am rejecting God's wisdom and sovereignty in creating me. God created me with love for his purpose. I did not have a say in or choice of how I wanted to be created. All I know is that I am not an accident and God had a plan in creating me. I always wanted to belong to God's family but the whole idea of being baptized and going to church and facing all the questions and preaching of disgrace about my sexuality made me postpone and delay this next step that I had to take eventually. I know that I became part of the human family by my first birth but I will become a member of God's family by my second birth. God has given me the privilege of being born again so that I could be a member of God's family. I know if I take this next step I will be able to take my relationship with God to the next level and obviously there are many benefits of being in God's family. I know that baptism alone does not make me a member of God's family only faith in Christ does that. Baptism shows that I am a part of God's family. I know it is not an optional ritual to be delayed or postponed. It is an act of initiation, not something I should put off until I am spiritually mature. I must no longer delay baptism, I must do it as soon as possible and I trust that God will give me strength to face those negative comments in church. I will be doing all of this for my God. This one is for you my Lord, this one is for you my father, my friend.

Relationships to me are what life is all about. I invest a lot of my precious time in all my relationships. I give all of my love to my God, myself, my family, in that particular order. At the moment I have all the time I need and we have a ritual, every Sunday after church I meet with my family for lunch. There is always a lot of serious discussion, joking around, praying for the future or just reminiscing about good memories. God knows I look forward to those Sunday sessions. I love them so much; we get to bond and know each other better. I used to have a lot of friends, but not anymore. One thing for sure is that God is my number one friend; I will definitely give my Lord my time and my loyalty.

My love life is at a complete standstill. I guess I am not that lucky when it comes to that department but eventually I would love to have a lifetime partner, someone I will love completely and someone who will love me as much as I love them. Life is all about love. Whenever I get the opportunity to help anyone I do it. Love cannot be learned in isolation, you have to be around people that are irritating, imperfect, frustrating. I use all my time to love although sometimes it is hard to give love to those unhappy, frustrating and irritating people because I know love is the number one priority in my life. Sometimes I get so busy and pre-occupied with making a living, going to work, paying my bills and accomplishing goals. My schedule becomes overloaded, I start cutting back on giving the time, energy and attention that loving relationships require. I often act as if relationships are something to be squeezed into my schedule and I make all my other tasks the point of my life, which they are not. Now I know it is not what I do, but how much love I put into it that matters. The more time I give to something the more I reveal its importance and value to me because the importance of things can be measured by how much time I invest in them. They say that if you want to know a person's priorities, just look at how they use their time. I must say I use my time very effectively. I always spend time with my Lord, myself and my family, my friends and maybe one day I will spend time with my spiritual partner. I am effective with my time by being selective; I have got my priorities straight. Time is my most precious gift because I only have a set amount of it. I can make more money but unfortunately I cannot make more time. When I give someone my time, I know that I am giving them a portion of my life that I will never get back. My time is my life; that is why the greatest gift I can give to someone is my time. Relationships to me are important and I show this by my investing my time in them because I know they take time and effort and the best way to spell love is T-I-M-E. Giving attention says – I value you enough to give you my time. I will always be there for people who need my time, I will help them and giving them my time and I hope I won't be too late because sometimes we postpone or delay to give our time because I think some people are attention seekers. I will delay no more I will give my time when it is needed most. It is not about money, it is not about things, it is about me giving my time to somebody that needs my time and it is not that they need attention only. They want me, my eyes, my ears, my love, my advice, my presence, my touch, my smell, my laugh, my sense of humor, my focus and nothing else can take the place of that. I won't be too late one day to offer my love. We all want people that we love and have relationships with to surround us when life on earth is ending. In our final moments is when we realize that relationships are what life is all about. So the best use of life is love, the best expression of love is time, the best time is now.

I have been avoiding getting baptized and going to church for some time now but I guess that is why I felt I was sliding off with my spiritual maturity. I thought that having a relationship with my God was enough but it is more than that. The church issue keeps popping up and since I am truly committed to my God there is no way of running from it, I have to do it. I have to do it as soon as possible; I have to belong to a church because I cannot do this on my own. This one is for you my God. I was created for community, fashioned for fellowship and formed for a family and no one can fulfill God's purpose by themselves. Following Christ includes belonging, not just believing. I was created for a special role but I will miss this second purpose of my life if I am not attached to a local church. I will discover my role in life through my relationship with others. I must admit I was ignorant and a little bit arrogant because I thought I really did not need to go to church but still believed that I could be a good Christian. I hated the idea of having committed and active in a church and everyone knowing my business. I liked the idea of hopping from one church to another without any identity or accountability. If people asked me, why do you or where do you go to church, I would tell them I was still looking for the perfect church to accommodate my beliefs because I did believe in my ancestors and I would start going on about church politics. Now I know I will keep looking but I will never find a perfect church because there is no such thing as a perfect church, it does not exist, period! I believe that soon I will belong to a church and it will find me and it won't be perfect. It will be good for me to belong to a church because I will learn how to get along in God's family; it's where I will practice unselfish sympathetic love. As the participating member I will learn to care about others and share the experience of others. I will experience the truth of being connected with and dependent on other church goers. I will be able to build my spiritual muscle by being a fully active participator, not a passive spectator. God has a unique role for me to play in his family, waiting just for me and I know he has gifted me for this role. I will be able to discover, develop and use all my gifts in God's family. It will keep me from backsliding and I will get all the support that I need. God made the church specially to help me fulfill the five purposes he has for my life. He created the church to meet my five deepest needs which are:

    1. purpose to live for
    2. people to live with
    3. principle to live by
    4. a profession to live out
    5. a profession to live on

A church is the only place that can fulfill all my needs. I need to join one because God wants me to love real people, not ideal people. He wants me to love imperfect sinners just like he does. I know myself that I am not perfect but guess what, God still loves me. I became a Christian by committing myself to Christ. Now I need to become a church member by committing myself to a specific group of believers. The first decision saved my soul from sin (salvation), the second will give me companionship. I will get the experience of sharing my life with others (fellowship).

I love the sound of sharing and companionship. I have experienced that in small doses with my friends but at the end I was disappointed with some of them. I had a lot of friends and I thought I could share everything with them, all my happiness and all my pain and I was loyal to each and every one of them. It was so genuine, heart-to-heart, sometimes gut-level sharing. We were honest about who we were and what was happening in our lives. We shared our hurt, revealed our feelings, confessed our failures, disclosed our doubts, admitted our fears, acknowledged our weaknesses. The experiences were mutual; we could depend on each other. There was always mutual accountability, mutual encouragement, mutual serving and mutual honoring. We would make every effort to do what lead to peace and the mutual uplifting of each other morally. We would offer each other sympathy by really entering into ordeals and sharing the pain of others and would really understand what the other was going through and feeling. I never felt openness like that in my life. We were tight and nobody could separate us, we were there for each other in times of deep crisis, grief and doubt and I believe that is when we would offer mercy to each other and be willing to receive it from each other because we all stumble and fall and require help getting back on track.

As you may know, once a group of friends becomes larger than about ten people, someone stops participating – usually the quietest person – and a few people will usually start to dominate the group. I stopped participating because most of the time I would feel totally out and ask myself, who are these people? Everyone now was starting to be superficial; it turned into surface level chit-chat instead of an atmosphere of honesty and humility. There was pretending, role playing, politicking, superficial politeness and shallow conversation. People wore masks, keeping their guard up and acting as if everything were rosy in their lives. These attitudes were the death of our real friendships. I thought I would never have the pleasure of experiencing sharing my life with a group of people, except my family of course. I found I could get companionship if only I went to church and got myself a group of believers that I could experience fellowship with, and of course size matters; the smaller the group the better, I am talking from experience here. I need to experience all the wonders that come with fellowship; the authenticity, mutuality, sympathy and mercy. God warns though that I cannot have fellowship without forgiveness. I never hold grudges anymore, well probably not for that long now, I am still working at it. I have to work harder though because I know bitterness and resentment always destroy fellowship because we are imperfect, sinful people, we end up hurting each other when we are together for a long enough time. Sometimes we hurt each other intentionally and sometimes unintentionally, but either way it takes a massive amount of mercy and grace to create and maintain fellowship. I must make allowance for other people's faults and forgive people who offend me. I must remember that the Lord forgave me, so I must forgive others and also try to remember that I will never be asked to forgive someone else more than God has already forgiven me.

When someone hurts me now I know I have got a choice – it is either I use my energy and emotions for retaliation or for resolution. I cannot do both, unfortunately. Sometimes I was reluctant to show mercy to people because I did not understand the difference between trust and forgiveness. Forgiveness is letting go of the past, trust has to do with future behavior. Forgiveness must be immediate, whether or not a person asks for it; trust must be rebuilt over time. Trust requires a track record, if someone hurts me repeatedly I am commanded by God to forgive them instantly but I am not expected to trust them immediately and I am not expected to continue allowing them to hurt me, they must prove they have changed over time. So yes, I need the support of a small group that offers both encouragement and accountability. Luckily I have that for now, my family and my dear friends, I just need church members.

This fellowship has made me hungry to experience the authenticity, mutuality sympathy and mercy of real fellowship. I just cannot wait! I love the idea and I know this is an essential part of my life that I cannot overlook. I am pleased to know that this fellowship I will be getting into will be able to take my frankness. I hope they are ready for me, I sincerely hope so because I am honest, I speak the truth, I do not sugarcoat or ignore an issue if it is bothering me. I refuse to remain silent whilst others are harming themselves or doing something wrong. Most people have no one in their lives who loves them enough to tell them the truth. I do not fear to speak my mind, fear does not sabotage me because I am one person who cannot just sit there and watch when somebody's life is falling apart and hope it will go away or hope that they will fight their own battles, I believe that people should sometimes fight their own fights, however if I see a good fight I always get in on it without asking questions and help them out to fight. I am not afraid of confrontations and that I guess most of my friends cannot handle, because they will always try to sugar coat an issue in order to preserve a false sense of peace. Mr Don't Rock the Boat will jump in and try to smooth everyone's ruffled feathers. The issue will never be resolved and they will act as if everything is normal or nothing happened. That is the most frustrating thing for me because everyone knows about the problem but no one talks about it openly. This creates a sick environment of secrets where gossip thrives. So yes, I was straightforward. I still am and I cannot pretend any more. I speak the truth and I apologize if I come out as being strong or harsh or even disrespectful but this is me. Take it or leave it.

Another thing that people do not get is that I have to disagree sometimes with people that I love dearly. In fact the tunnel of conflict is the passageway to intimacy in any relationship. But when you avoid it you grow apart. You must always handle it correctly and you will grow closer to each other and you will be able to face and resolve your differences. I know that my frankness is not a license to say anything I want, wherever and whenever I want. It is not rudeness because I know there is a right time and right way to do everything.

Thoughtless words leave lasting wounds, I must work on my approach, I must be more gentle, sincere, loving and respectful when I confront people. Another trait of mine is stubbornness and pride and these can destroy companionship faster than anything else. Pride builds walls between people, so I must learn to be humble because humility builds bridges. I must always have a humble attitude because God opposes the proud but gives grace to the humble. Some of the ways to develop humility is by admitting my weaknesses, by being patient with others weaknesses, by being open to correction and by pointing the spot light on others. I try not to act self-important and I enjoy the company of ordinary people and I do not think I know it all because I know nothing. I give more honor to others than to myself and I am more interested in other people's lives, how they do it or have done it. I am not so much more into my own life anymore it is not about me! I am not thinking less of myself, I am thinking of myself less and lately I think more about other people and I am focusing on how I should serve them. I know everybody is different and I am more considerate when it comes to other people's feelings and I try to be patient with people who irritate me. I am considerate of other people's doubts and fears. I must work on my courtesy skills because another part of courtesy is not down playing on other people's doubts. Just because I do not fear something it does not make it an invalid feeling, I must be the one person that they feel safe with and trust, and know that they can share their doubts and fears with me without being judged.

The truth is we all have quirks and annoying traits but community has nothing to do with compatibility, the basic for fellowship is our relationship with God and one key to courtesy is to understand where people are coming from. Discover their history; find out what they have been through. When you do that you will be more understanding. Instead of thinking about how far they still have to go, I will think about how far they have come in spite of their hurt. When I find my fellowship group I will defend and protect them like my family and I will excel in treating and showing them respect. We will be a family.

The last thing I must learn is confidentiality because I cannot keep some things to myself, I find it so hard. I always feel the need to share. Sometimes it is so unnecessary but after I share it I feel so much lighter. Well that is another fault of mine and I guess I can say it is my weakness. So it will be a little bit difficult for me because confidentiality will mean that what is shared in the group needs to stay in the group and the group needs to deal with it and not gossip, especially when it is thinly disguised as a prayer request for someone else. I have heard enough of those prayer requests to last me a lifetime. Last but not least it will take frequency and that! I can live with because I know that relationships take time to build. I will have to see them often in order to build a genuine fellowship. I will have to spend time with them, a lot of time to build a deep relationship.

Chapter 6

You can call me a peacemaker because I am never afraid of conflict. I am not a doormat. I refuse to back down on issues I strongly believe in, I always stand my ground. I have got a backbone, as they call it. God wants me to value relationships and make the effort to maintain them, instead of writing them off whenever there is a rift. Blessed are those who work for peace and those who actively seek to resolve conflict. I want to have the ability to get along with everyone and enhance my skills on conflict resolution, so that I can maintain and restore all my relationships.

1.   I discuss the problem with God by praying about the conflict first instead of gossiping to a friend. Pray! Pray! Pray!

2.   I take the initiative. It does not matter whether I am the offender or the offended. I make the first move so that it is sorted out quickly and that reduces spiritual damage to me.

3.   I sympathize with other people's feelings; I use my ears more than my mouth. Patience comes from wisdom and wisdom comes from hearing, the perspective of others and people do not care what we know until they know that we care.

4.   I confess my part of the conflict by admitting my own mistakes not making excuses or shifting the blame. I own up to any part I have played in the conflict, accept responsibility for my mistakes and ask for forgiveness.

5. I always try to attack the problem, not the person. I choose my words wisely and try not to get cross. I always try to fix the problem, instead of trying to fix the blame, avoid belittling, comparing, labeling, insulting, condescending and being sarcastic. A gentle response defuses anger, but a sharp tongue kindles a temper fire. So in resolving conflict, how you say it is as vital as what you say.

6. I cooperate as much as possible. I try to do everything possible on my part to live in peace with everybody, although peace always has a price tag. Sometimes it will cost me my pride which will be difficult for me. My weakness is that I get so self-centered sometimes and I know I have got a lot of pride but I always do my best to compromise and adjust to others and show preference to what they need. I know I will be blessed when I can show people how to cooperate instead of competing or fighting. That is when I discovered who I am and my place in God's family.

7. I emphasize reconciliation not resolution because I cannot expect everyone to agree about everything. Reconciliation focuses on the relationship, while resolution focuses on the problem. I focus on reconciliation because the minute I do that, the problem loses significance and often becomes irrelevant. I can re-establish my relationships even when we are unable to resolve our differences. As they say, let's agree to disagree. The diamond looks different from different angles. God expects unity, not uniformity and we can walk arm-in-arm without seeing eye-to-eye on every issue, but that does not mean we must give up on finding a solution. I continue discussing or debating the issues but I do it in a spirit of harmony. Reconciliation means we bury the hatchet, not necessarily the issue.

I was created to become like Christ. God has made me in his image and likeness. It is a great privilege and it gives me dignity. God wants me to be godly, taking on his values, attitude and character. God's ultimate goal for my life on earth is not comfort but character development. He wants me to grow up spiritually and become like Christ. It is good to know that becoming like Christ does not mean losing my personality or becoming a mindless clone. God created my uniqueness so he certainly won't destroy it. Becoming Christ-like is all about transforming my character, not my personality. Every time when I get frustrated by my circumstances I ask myself these questions: Why am I having such a difficult time? Why is this happening to me? It is because every time I forget that character development is one of God's purposes for my life. Every time I forget, God reminds me and tells me that my life is supposed to be difficult. This reminder enables me to grow and develop my character and remember earth is not heaven.

I was one of those Christians who misinterpreted Jesus' promise of the abundant life. I still pray to Jesus for abundant life, that is perfect health, a comfortable lifestyle, constant happiness, good relationships, full realization of my dreams and instant relief from my pain and problem through faith and prayer. These are all the things that I prayed for or wrote in my journal when I wanted abundant life. I expected my life to be fulfilled and easy. I wanted God to serve me in my selfish pursuit of personal fulfillment but God is not my servant. I was severely disillusioned – I was living in denial of reality. This was actually a shock for me and I guess it will take some time to sink in. This life it is not about me at all, I only exist for God's purpose. God is working in me, giving me the desire to obey him and the power to do what pleases him. I must cooperate with the Holy Spirit's work by having faith. The Holy Spirit releases power the moment I take a step of faith. God waits for me to act first. I must not wait to feel powerful or confident; I must go ahead in my weakness and do something right in spite of my fears and feelings. I must make every effort in my growth toward becoming like Jesus. I won't sit around and wait for it to happen. There are three responsibilities in becoming like Christ.

1. Let go of old ways of acting;
2. Change the way I think, letting the spirit change my way of thinking;
3. Put on the character of Christ by developing new godly habits

God always uses his word, people and circumstances to mold us. Mostly he uses his people to perform his good deeds so that we can depend on each other for fellowship. He wants us to grow together, isolation is a no-no. I must be around other people and interact with them. I need to be part of a church and community; it is all about love; loving God and loving others. Becoming like Christ is a long, slow process of growth. It is neither instant nor automatic. It is a gradual progressive development that will take the rest of my life. I am a work in progress. I was confused in my life with different misinterpretations of the Bible and different books that I read; especially self-help books and I ignored the simple truth that God is far more interested in building my character than in anything else. I worried when God seemed so silent and distant on specific issues such as, what am I good at? What is my talent? What career should I choose? The truth is there are many different careers that could be God's will for my life. What God cares about most is that whatever I do, I do in a

Christ-like manner. God is far more interested in what I am than in what I do; he is into my character not my career. I am a human being not a human doing. Jesus did not die on the cross just so I could live a comfortable, well-adjusted life. His purpose is far deeper; he wants to make me like himself before he takes me to heaven. I need to grow, I have decided to grow and I am persisting in growing. I do not totally understand all the implications but I have made my decision. I fully commit myself to Jesus, I am ready now and I am not afraid to commit myself anymore. I have made my choice, it is done. I know that God will do his part as long as I do my part. I feel better by just knowing that I will continue to work out my salvation with fear and trembling, for it is God who works in me and act according to his good purpose. This is between me and the Holy Spirit, God's spirit works with me, not just in me. This for me is a puzzle; I have all the pieces, all I need to do now is to work out the puzzle and put all the pieces together. God has given me a new life. Now I am responsible for developing it with fear and trembling. I am taking my spiritual growth seriously. I must change my auto-pilot, starting with the way I think because my life is shaped by the way I think. I must develop the mind of Christ and adopt the way he thinks. I must stop thinking immature thoughts which are self-centered and self-seeking. I will always remember this is not about me. I must start thinking maturely, which means focusing on and thinking about others, not myself. I must always think of their good and try to help them by doing what pleases them; even Jesus did not try to please himself. It is never too late to start growing; spiritual growth is a process of replacing lies with truth.

I got myself a Bible because God's word is the spiritual nourishment I must have to fulfill my purpose. I never take it for granted; I consider it as essential to my life as food. I must abide by God's word by accepting its authority. The Bible has the first and last word in my life. I feel that this will be an interesting journey for me because there are some issues that I strongly disagree with in the Bible and I cannot wait to find out more. All my life I made choices based on unreliable authorities like culture because everyone is doing it, tradition because we have always done it that way, reason because it seemed logical or emotion because it just felt right. All of them were wrong. What I need in my life is an authoritative standard that will never lead me in the wrong direction and only God's word meets that need. It will correct me and show me how to live my life. I must absorb its truth because believing in the Bible is just not enough, I must fill my mind with it so that the Holy Spirit can transform me with the truth. There are five ways I do this:

1.   Receive by listening and accepting it with an open, receptive attitude and I must always check my attitude, especially for pride, any time I feel that I am not getting it.
2.   Read the Bible regularly – which means it must be a daily habit.
3.   Research or study by writing my questions and insights
4.   Remember by memorizing scriptures.
5.   Reflect in my mind. I must apply its principles by practicing all these five steps. I must become the doer of the word. The Bible was not given to increase our knowledge but to change our lives. Correct me if I am wrong but I think I am getting it now. It is all about me having a relationship with God and me having relationship with others and developing my character and growing up.

Chapter 7

God has a purpose behind every problem that I am facing right this moment. The circumstances and problems I have now. They are all for my character development. It is not a nice feeling to be me right now, but it brings relief to know this too shall pass. My life is a series of problems twenty-four-seven. The drama never ends. Every time I solve one, another one is waiting to take its place. Not all of them are major but all of them are vital in God's growth process for me.

In my life problems are normal and God uses them to draw me closer to him. He wants to rescue my crushed spirit. Right now I am in great pain; I am suffering, my heart is broken, I am disappointed, I feel abandoned, nothing is going my way, I feel out of control. I have got no plan B, I am out of options and I shall call these dark times "Winter Light".

These dark days give me the most profound and intimate experiences of worship in my whole life. I never felt this close to God until this winter light. I always told people that I have a relationship with God but now I think I have an intimate relationship with God. In this winter light I learned to pray the most authentic, heartfelt, honest-to-God prayers. Now I know what Jesus did for me. I learned things about God in this winter light that I would not have learned any other way. You will never know that God is all you need until God is all you have got. This statement is so true because the first thing I did when I was in great pain was to turn to God alone, he is the man! He is the one in control of my life, so everything bad that happens to me God intends to use for my good even when others mean it for bad. Everything that happens to me has spiritual significance, everything!

I know now that this winter light produces patience and patience produces character. I am full of fear and I tremble just thinking that God will take me through the same experiences Jesus went through, including loneliness, temptation, stress, criticism, rejection and many other problems. I just hope crucifixion is not included in those other problems. I will go through exactly what Christ went through, and thankfully God will be there with me. If I go through the winter light with him, then I will certainly go through the good times with him.

I used to become bitter rather than better and never grow up when problems did not automatically produce what God intended. I am blessed to know that I must remember that God's plan is good; he really knows what is best for me and has my best interests at heart. His plans are for me to prosper and not to harm me in any way. He plans to give me hope and a future, a bright one for that matter. I have no fear about other people intending to harm me because now I know God will change the bad intention for good. It is for my own good that I am having such hard times right now. God is doing what is best for me at this moment, he is training me to live God's holy best. What I need to do right now is to stay focused on God's plan, not my pain or problems and this is how Jesus endured the pain on the cross. The secret of endurance is to remember that my pain is temporary but my reward will be eternal. What I suffer now is nothing compared to the glory he will give me later, so I must focus on the end result, I rejoice and give thanks to all my circumstances. Thank you my Lord for using my problems to fulfill your purpose. I rejoice in you my Lord because I know that we are both going through this pain together. I am glad to know that you are with me all the way. I am not on my own; I refuse to give up no matter what comes my way. I am patient and persistent. I will let the process go on until my endurance is fully developed because I want to become a man of mature character with no weak spots. I feel that this day will come sooner than I expect. I cannot wait until when winter light comes to an end.

I now ask God: What do you want me to learn? What is it that I am supposed to do now? Then I trust God and keep on doing what is right. There are no more, "why me?" questions anymore. I am done with it. If not me who else? I won't give up because now is the time to grow up. Growing through temptations will not be an easy task, but I know every temptation will be an opportunity for me to do good. When the Holy Spirit controls my life, he will produce these kinds of fruits in me: love, joy, peace, patience, kindness, goodness, faithfulness, gentleness and self-control. This is a beautiful description of Jesus; these fruits will mature and ripen slowly. God develops the fruit of spirit in my life by allowing me to experience circumstances in which I will be tempted to express the exact opposite quality. Character development always involves a choice and temptation provides that opportunity God teaches us to love by putting some unlovely people around us; he teaches us real joy in the midst of sorrow. When we turn to him, happiness depends on external circumstances but joy is based on my relationship with God.

I learned real peace by choosing to trust God in circumstances in which I am tempted to worry or be afraid. Patience is developed in circumstances like mine in which I am forced to wait and I am tempted to be angry or have a short fuse. God uses the opposite situation of each fruit to allow me a choice. I cannot claim to be good if I have never been tempted to be bad. I cannot claim to be faithful if I have never had the opportunity to be unfaithful. Integrity is built by defeating the temptation to be dishonest, humility grows when I refuse to be prideful and endurance develops every time I reject the temptation to give up. Temptation works in four ways.

Step one: Satan will identify a desire inside me and then start suggesting with a thought that I end up giving in to that desire and fulfill it in a wrong way at the wrong time. Satan will whisper and say it is a shortcut! I deserve it! I should have it now! It will be exciting, comforting, or it will make me feel better. When I am at work there is a lot of temptation to take something.

Step two: Satan will try to get me to doubt what God has said about sin. I will always have doubts when thinking that God helps those who help themselves. I mean God wants me to be happy or, he loves me and he really wants me to have whatever? God did not mean this prohibition for me.

Step three: He will try to deceive me and tell me that I can get away with it, nobody will notice a thing. It will solve my problems, besides everyone is doing it, it is only a little sin, but a little sin is like being a little pregnant; it will eventually show itself.

Step four: He will finally make me disobey my Lord. I will finally act on the thought I have been toying with in my mind. What began as an idea gets birthed into behavior I will eventually give in to. Whatever got to my attention causes me to believe Satan's lies and fall into his trap. I understand now how temptation works but I need to overcome it by refusing to be intimidated. I must never feel ashamed by being tempted because if I do that I will never outgrow temptation. I must consider temptation as a compliment because Satan does not have to tempt those who are already doing his evil work, they are already his.

Temptation is a sign that Satan hates me. I know it's not a sin to be tempted and I know I won't be able to avoid it completely in my life. Now I won't be surprised, shocked or discouraged by it, because it only becomes a sin when I give in to it. I recognize my patterns of temptation and now I am prepared for them. I stay alert, especially when I am at work because that is where I am more vulnerable. The devil knows my weakness and he is constantly working to get me into those circumstances. Now I will protect myself by watching where I am going. I avoid evil and walk straight ahead. I won't go one step off the right way, so help me God! There is always a way out, sometimes it may feel too overpowering for me too bear but I know now that is a lie of Satan, because God has promised never to allow more on me than he puts within me to handle any circumstance or temptation. I can overcome anything that comes my way but God warns that when it comes to temptation I must never get too cocky or overconfident. I must do my part by praising the four biblical keys to defeating temptation:

1. I must refocus my attention on something else, just change the channel of my mind and get interested in another idea. I must totally ignore it and once my mind is on something else, the temptation loses its power. I must do whatever is necessary to turn my attention to something else always and think about Jesus. I must be selective and choose carefully what I think about. This will take me a lifetime of practice, but with the help of the Holy Spirit, I can reprogram my mind.

2. I must reveal my struggle to God, friends and support groups, because if I confess to someone this will be the beginning of my healing; willpower and personal resolutions are not enough. I will be better off having a friend than being

all alone because a friend can pray for me, encourage me and hold me accountable.

3. I must resist the devil by using the word of God as my weapon and memorizing scriptures is absolutely essential to defeating temptation. I must memorize one verse a week for the rest of my life.

4. I must realize my vulnerability and always know that given the right circumstances any of us are capable of any sin. I must never let down my guard and think I am beyond temptation. I am not exempted and I must always avoid putting myself in tempting situations and always remember that it is easier to stay out of temptation than to get out of it. This will take time. All that I have learned so far will take time and a lot of practice and I have to be patient, take it one day at a time. There are absolutely no shortcuts to maturity, I cannot rush the development of Christ-like character. I worry about how fast I grow but God is concerned about how strong I grow. I am such in a hurry to grow but God is never in a hurry with my life, I admit I did not open my life to Christ the first time he knocked on my door, I was resistant and defensive because I felt that if I opened the door for him it meant I would be giving all my life to him. I was scared by the whole idea but now I know the truth. I gave my life to the Lord and I want him to use my life for his purpose.

It took this winter light for me to really open my life to Christ but I know that this is only the beginning. This is a small step. There is a lot that I have to give that I am not even aware of. I have to surrender every day of my life, twenty-four-seven because I can only give God as much of me as I understand at that moment, and that is okay with me. I know Jesus will take over more and more territory until all of my life is completely his. This won't be easy for me – there will be struggle and battle but the outcome will never be in doubt. God has promised that to me, since he began good work in me, he will carry it on to completion. My final goal is to be Christ-like, but my journey to get there will last a lifetime. So far I have seen that this journey involves believing through worship, belonging through fellowship and becoming through discipleship. Every day God wants me to become a little more like him. I have begun to live the new life, in which I am being made new and I am slowly becoming like the one who made me. I love speed, I want things to happen fast, here and now, but God is more interested in my strength and stability than swiftness. My growth will be gradual. My life will slowly and gradually becomes brighter and more beautiful as God enters my life and I become like him. God wants to develop me slowly. He is doing it little by little so that I will not be overwhelmed. I am a slow learner so I often have to relearn a lesson several times to really get it. The problem recurs and I think, not again! I have already learned that. This reminds me of all the accidents with my car but it took me some time to really get it – God knows better. After my car accidents I would quickly forget the lesson that God was teaching me and soon go back to my old ways of doing things, reverting to my old patterns of behavior. That is why they were recurring several times until I got it. I really needed repeated exposure because I am a slow learner. I still have a lot to learn and there is no quick solution since most of my problems and all my bad habits took years to develop. It would be unrealistic of me to expect them to go away immediately and no prayer will instantly undo the damage of many years. It requires the hard work of removal and replacement. My old habits and patterns need to be removed and replaced by brand new ones.

I am afraid to humbly face the truth about myself and I know that the truth will set me free. I still get miserable, fearing what I might discover if I honestly face my character, but I have done it and I found out that I was living in the prison of denial. I am so glad I did that now, I can begin to work on my faults. I did it with a humble and teachable attitude so that I can be able to grow. The growing part is often painful and scary. I must let go of old ways in order to experience the new. As the say: there is no growth without change, no change without fear or loss and no loss without pain. I fear these losses and I just do not want to let go sometimes, even if my old ways were damaging my health or putting me at risk of having lung cancer. Now I am talking about my smoking habit. It is so hard for me to quit because I feel smoking helps me think things through when I get stressed. Smoking calms me down. When I wake up I light up a fag and now I am so comfortable with it and it is really hard and painful every time I decide to quit. Something bad will happen to me and I will get stressed and relapse. Smoking cigarettes is so familiar to me but I won't give up; I will keep trying and I know soon my body and lungs will be smoke free.

I often build my identity around my defects and say it is just the way I am. I unconsciously worry that if I let go of my habit, my hurt or my weakness, who will I be? This fear is really slowing down my growth. Habits take time to develop and I must start practicing the habit of a Christ-like character, like showing kindness without thinking, and always being honest. I must devote my life to my fellow people so that everyone can see my progress. I must slow down and take it easy; there is no need to hurry. I must cooperate with God in the process by believing that God is working in my life even when I do not feel it. I must expect gradual improvement but I will still keep praying for a miracle to quit smoking, to wake up one day and not crave a cigarette. I won't be disappointed if the answer comes through a gradual change.

I keep a journal and I write everything I go through. Now I have to write down all the lessons I have learned. I decided to write down the insights and life lessons God teaches me about myself, about my life, relationships and everything else. I guess this will be my part two of my book. I record these so that I can review and remember them and pass them on to the next generation. I must relearn lessons so that I don't forget them. I review my spiritual journal regularly, especially on December 31st of every year. When people are partying a storm, I am on my own reading and reviewing my journal and the lessons I have learned for that year. It has become one of my rituals. I do this so that I can spare myself a lot of unnecessary pain and heartache and repetition of teachings and circumstances. I have learnt to be patient with God and myself because God's timetable is rarely the same as mine. I am often in a hurry when God is not and I feel frustrated with the slow progress that I am making with my life but I remember God is never in a hurry, he is always on time, his timing is always perfect. He will use my entire lifetime to prepare me for my role in eternity. I must just be patient with my God and let him do his job so that I can become mature and well-developed. I won't get discouraged. I will always remember how far I have come, not just how far I have to go. I am not where I want to be at present, but neither am I where I used to be. God is not finished with me yet so I will keep moving forward. Even the snail reached the ark by persevering. Perseverance is the mother of success! That is me, my name, surely that must mean something. This proves I was not an accident and God made me for his purpose, but of course I have to work on my patience big time!

God designed me to make a difference with my life. Now is the time to accept my assignment and serve others. I was created to add to life on earth not take from it. God wants me to give something back. Whenever I serve others in any way, I will be serving God and fulfilling one of his purposes. I am here on this planet for a special assignment – God saved me in order for me to serve him. He wanted me to do all his holy work here on earth school. I was saved for service. I must serve God with joy and deep gratitude for what he has done for me. I owe him my life; my past has been forgiven, my present is given a meaning and my future is secured. I am offering myself as a living sacrifice to God, dedicated to his service. My heart has been saved – I have lots of love for others. Now I am healed I can help others and I am blessed to be a blessing. I am saved to serve and not to sit around and wait for heaven. I am called to full-time Christian service regardless of my job or career. This is my calling, to serve God. I always thought that only pastors, nuns, monks or special kinds of people get this calling but I know now that every Christian is called to service. Now I belong to God, I am commanded to serve God and make time to serve and give my life to others. I must keep on learning and act on what I know and practice, what I claim to believe. God wants me to learn to love and serve others unselfishly; he is preparing me for eternity. I am fully alive when I am helping others, even if it is just a small thing. It is a small part I play in their lives, but it makes me more significant.

Chapter 8

God wants to use me to make a difference in his world. He wants to work through me and what matters is not the duration of my life but the donation of it. It's not how long I lived, but how I lived before God created me. He decided what role he wanted me to play on earth. He planned exactly how he wanted me to serve him and then he shaped me for those tasks. I am the way I am today because I was made for a specific ministry (service). God gave me abilities, interests, talents, gifts, personality and life experiences for me to use them for his glory. I must understand and identify these factors so that I can discover God's will for my life. I am a wonderfully complex combination of many different factors.

I must discover and understand my SHAPE – that is S, spiritual gifts; H, heart; A, abilities; P, personality; E, experiences. Firstly I must unwrap my spiritual gifts because I know that an unopened gift is worthless. Honestly I do not know what my spiritual gifts are yet. Maybe God has not given them to me yet because I know I cannot earn my spiritual gifts or deserve them, they have to be a gift from God. I hope one day I get to unwrap and open my spiritual gifts so that I can use them with all of the other factors in my shape for the ministry (service) God intends me to have. I should do it with enthusiasm, I should do it with all my heart, I should love what I do. No one has to motivate or challenge me or even check up on me. I must do it for the sheer enjoyment, I should not need rewards, applause or payment. I must enjoy it and cannot wait to do it the next day. This is how I know when I am serving God from my heart. I will be good at what I do because God wired me to be good at what I do and love it and be effective. My passion will drive me to perfection and I will excel because I will be doing what I love and care about, I will be doing what I love to do all for passion, not duty or profit. I will be expressing my heart and it is not about money or things, it is about meaning in my life. I am aiming for the better life, me serving God in a way that expresses my heart. This one is for you my Lord.

I was born with natural talents so I must make sure I identify them. I have always envied those people who knew their talents at an early age and I wonder when I will un-tap my talents. It is a tough one for me but the truth is I have dozens if not hundreds of unrecognized and unused abilities lying doormat inside me. I must identify them soon, so help me Lord because all of them come from God and God has given me the ability to do certain things well. My abilities must all be used for God's glory. I am the only person on earth who can use my abilities. No one else can play my role because they do not have the unique shape that God has given me. I must seriously examine what I am good at doing and what I am not good at. On the other hand the abilities I do have are a strong indication of what God wants me to do with my life, so I can make a safe assumption that God's plan for my life includes that skill somehow. I found God in me and I love him fiercely. God does not waste abilities he matches our calling and our capabilities. My abilities were not given to me just to make a living, God gave them to me for my ministry (service). I have a unique personality and I must use it for God's ministry. My personality will affect how and where I use my spiritual gifts and abilities. I must always be me and not try to be someone else. I can learn from others but I must filter what I learn through my own shape. I must employ all my experiences by examining my family experiences, educational experiences, vocational experiences, spiritual experiences, ministry experiences and painful experiences. The truth is the very experiences that I have resented most in my life, they're one's that I wanted to hide and forget about. Those experiences will be the ones God will want me to use in order to help others. Experience is not what happens or has happened to me, it is what I do with it. I won't waste my pain anymore; I will definitely use it to help others. I will be most effective when I use my spiritual gifts and abilities in the areas my heart desires and in a way that best expresses my personality and experiences.

What I am is God's gift to me and what I do with myself is my gift to God. I must go ahead and be what I was made to be starting now and God deserves my best. God does not want me to worry about abilities I do not have, instead he wants me to focus on the talents he has given me to use. I must discover my shape, learn to accept and enjoy it and then develop it to its fullest potential. I won't waste another day. I must start accessing my gifts and abilities by making a list and asking other people for their honest opinions, because my gifts and abilities will always be confirmed by others. I must always search for the truth and not fish for compliments. Another way for me to discover my gifts and abilities is to experiment with different areas of service. I must try doing things that I have never done before and never stop experimenting because this is the only way for me to find out what I am good at. I must always consider my heart and my personality by always asking myself these questions: What do I really enjoy doing most? When do I feel the most alive? What am I doing when I lose track of time? Do I like routine or variety? Do

I prefer serving in a team or by myself? Am I more introverted or extroverted? Am I more a thinker or a feeler? Which do I enjoy more, competing or cooperating? Again it will help to get feedback from those who know me best. I must always examine my experiences and extract the lessons I have learned by reviewing my life and thinking about how it has shaped me. Luckily for me I keep a journal and I can always go back to that. Now I am going to take an entire weekend for a life review, to retreat, just to pause and go back to my journals to see how God has worked in the various defining moments of my life and consider how he wants to use those lessons for me to help others. I should accept, enjoy and celebrate the shape God has given only to me. If only I could find out what God was thinking, because at this stage I am second guessing. I will run with patience the particular race that God has set before me and always focus on finishing my race. I have always taken my time doing my work well, I do my best and give it my all and I let it go and I do not compare myself to anyone else. It feels good and. I enjoy the personal satisfaction of having done my work so well. I always give myself a hug after a flight for a job well done!

I must always ignore those people who criticize me because they do not understand my shape and they will try to get me to conform to what they think I should be doing. I should respond by avoiding comparisons, resisting exaggerations and seek only God's commendations. I must just keep on developing my shape by cultivating my gifts and talents, keeping my heart aflame, growing my character and personality and broadening my experiences so that I can be effective in my service. If I fail to use what I have been given I will lose it, but if I fail to see what the ability I have got, then God will definitely increase it. I must put these abilities to work practice! Practice! Practice! I must stretch myself and learn all I can. I must take advantage of every training opportunity to develop my shape and sharpen my serving skills.

I serve God by serving others and I must have the heart of a servant. I must get rid of this self-serving "me first" mentality. I need to have a servant's heart because without it, I will be tempted to use my shape for personal gain. To be like Jesus is to be a servant so I must prepare myself to do particular tasks or serve in ways for which I am not shaped. I will be servicing wherever I am needed at whichever moment. My servant's heart will reveal my maturity. I can only know if I have a servant's heart if I make myself available to serve. I must jump to volunteer in situations when I am needed and always be available. I must do what is needed, even when it is inconvenient. I must give up the right to control my schedule and allow God to interrupt it whenever he needs to and do whatever he wants to bring into my life. I pay attention to the needs of others and always seize the moment by looking for ways to meet the needs of others. Great opportunities to serve others never last long; they pass quickly and sometimes never return, so I take advantage of the moment without delay because I may only get one chance to serve that person. I begin by looking for small tasks that no one else wants to do and treat these little things as if they were great things because God is watching and I now live my life for an audience of one – that is my Lord. I try to do the best with what I have and just do what needs to be done, no excuses. God expects me to do what I can with what I have wherever I am because if I wait for perfect conditions I will never get anything done. Less than perfect service is always better than the best intention. I do every duty with equal dedication and do it with all my heart; the size of the tasks is irrelevant. Small tasks often show a big heart and great opportunities always disguise themselves in small tasks. I am willing to do anything needed. I am faithful to my service and always make sure that I finish what I start and am fully committed because faithful servants never retire from serving God.

I always maintain a low profile – try to avoid attention to myself and not show off because the most significant service is often the service that is unseen. This one is more like my character because I hate the limelight, in fact I avoid it when possible, I am content with quietly serving in the shadows. I changed my attitude and this required a mental shift because service starts in my mind. I think like a servant and servants think more about others than about themselves. Servants think like stewards not owners, servants think about their work, not what others are doing, servants base their identities in Christ, which means I must be willing to accept jobs that insecure people would consider beneath them. Servants think of ministry as an opportunity, not an obligation.

God loves to use weak people like me, imperfect people; ordinary people to do extraordinary things in spite of our weaknesses. I must admit my weaknesses. A weakness is any limitation that I inherited or have no power to change, like personality quirks or a talent, or intellectual limitation. If I want God to use me I must know who God is and know who I am. I must be content with my weaknesses and believe that God loves me and knows what is best for me. God specializes in turning weaknesses into strengths. He wants to take my greatest weakness and transform it. I must honestly share my weaknesses because the more I let down my guard, take off my mask and share my struggles, the more God will be able to use me in serving others. Service begins with vulnerability. It is risky but the benefits are worth the risk.

At some point in my life I must decide whether I want to impress or influence people. I can impress people from a distance but I must get close to influence them and when I do that, they will be able to see my flaws and that is okay because the most essential quality for leadership is not perfection, but credibility. People must be able to trust me or they won't follow me and credibility is built by not pretending to be perfect, but by being honest. God uses my weaknesses for his glory so from now on I am going to boast only about how weak I am and how great God is to use such weakness for his glory. Instead of posing as self-confident and invincible, I see myself as a trophy of grace. I was made for a mission and I will make it my mission to find out my mission and accept it because God has perfect timing. His timing is always impeccable. My ministry is my service to believers and also unbelievers. To introduce people to God is my fifth purpose. God created me to love him.

The first purpose is to be part of his family, the second purpose is to become like him, the third purpose to serve him, the fourth purpose is to tell others about him, and lastly the fifth purpose God has given me is a life message to share and introduce others to him. I have a storehouse of experiences and lessons I have learned that God wants to use to bring others into his family.

Chapter 9

My life message has four parts to it, that is:

<u>My testimony</u>: The story of how I began a relationship with Jesus.

<u>My life lessons</u>: The most important lessons God has taught me.

<u>My godly passions</u>: The issues God shaped me to care about most.

<u>My good news</u>: The message of salvation, that I must become a world class Christian and stay on track and balance God's five purposes for my life.

A thank you note to Miss Oprah Winfrey:

My life purpose statement is; God is the center of my life, I am going to live for him, I center my life around him because he is strong enough to hold me together when life starts breaking apart. I pray that God will be more and more at home in my heart, I worship him always so that he can be at the center of my life. Every time I am alone with God, I work on developing these character qualities in my life. The qualities are my patience, my love, my joy, my kindness, my goodness, my faithfulness, my gentleness and my self-control. I know it will take a lifetime to build Christ-like behavior and character. I am stumbling but I won't give up, I shall not be moved.

I started a gratitude journal and every day I have to write at least five things that I am grateful for. I have to be grateful for what I have so that I begin to see that I have more. It is a little thing but it also is a big thing, because if the only prayer I say is thank you, that is enough.

There is so much I could do and I do best when I surrender it to my God. If I am not sure of what to believe, I look around me. If I believe that this world is angry, cruel and bitter, it will be that way. So I look around me and see the people that surround me. Are they angry? Are they jealous? That is the reflection of my orientation towards the world, so I make sure I surround myself with people that will motivate, support, and cultivate me.

My life is filled with loving, caring and compassionate people and that is the reflection and that will not change orientation until I change. I stop and say thank you when I am in the middle of the biggest crisis of my life. The first thing I say is thank you for it, because I know that my faith is so strong that whatever it is, it is only there to teach me more about myself. Whatever it is I am going to come of it, I am going to come out on the other side and on the other side of every storm is a great sense of joy. Life is big!

I have the willingness to take risks with my own life, the willingness to live an enchanted life, a life where I do things that mean something, a willingness to see the other side of things. It is like turning up the volume of my life, not just turning it on, but turning it up! Life is big! We are as big as life; that is what we are – we make life small and think it is only our income. Life is big! We have it now, I mean this is it, let's do it. To see anger and bitterness and hardness disappear to be replaced by the gentle spirit of overflowing love is exciting, I celebrate me, Sifiso Perseverance Mpongose. They have wished for me and persevered and got me. I am unique, in the whole world there is only one me. There is only one person with my shape, with my talents, experiences and gifts. I am proud of what I am and that is why I am so happy with myself. I am stronger and happier than before. I always bounce back like a palm tree and do not stay down for long.

While life is not always the way we want it, no tragedy lasts forever, recovery and survival are in reach when I trust the Lord my father. No matter what has happened in the past that is over. No matter how much I wish the past had been different, I cannot change what has already happened. I do not mourn over what is done anymore, I rejoice knowing that there is still a future. I have abandoned the past and I am embracing the future. Yesterday is a cancelled cheque, tomorrow is a promissory note and today is cash. I use my cash to the last cent because life is very short. I am in the present and live each day to its fullest as if tomorrow will never come. I have realized that nothing is perfect, nothing is exactly right however I enjoy and appreciate what I have, not what I wish I had. I have learned to accept what life has for me. Prayer is asking for rain, hope is telling yourself that it will rain and faith is carrying an umbrella.

Recently I developed a neat idea. Someone suggested to me that life is not what I want, but what I have got. I am happy with that because I know now I have got the wisdom to know that certain things or circumstances in my life cannot be changed and I won't understand the reasons at the time. I have stopped looking for reasons, they will come in time. Life gets heavy for me and I wonder how I can cope with the load. Love does not hurt, love does not have to be profound or educated or dazzling, it just has to be there, steady, sure, even in the bad times. Be the change that you want to see. I always teach people how to treat me. I am a very quiet person and my silence speaks volumes. The first step to my wisdom is silence, the second is listening. I am an effective communicator because communication contributes indirectly to my happiness. It is the key to my love life, job, social life, family and interests. Communication is not just speaking well. I remember what I do not say verbally may sometimes contradict what I say; that is my body language.

Chapter 10

"MY LIFE LESSONS AND MY DEEPEST INSIGHTS" GOD
TEACHES ME ABOUT HIM, ABOUT MY TRUE SELF,
ABOUT MY LIFE HERE ON EARTH SCHOOL, MY
RELATIONSHIPS AND EVERYTHING ELSE…

2001 Lessons:

I was at the prime of my life. Two years working as a flight attendant, enjoying my life and independence to the fullest and having lots of fun and lots of friends. My focus was on saving for a car and waiting for my bond to be registered so that whatever change I was going to get from the seller, I would add to my savings for the deposit of my brand new first car. I was over indulging, partying too much and booking off sick a lot, abusing my sick leave, especially after my international flights off-days. My bond was finally registered after my birth date and I deposited the car for R24 000, 00.

I was a young, hot guy, everything was going my way. I was working hard at this time. I stayed with my partner but as soon as I got my car I did not give him the time of the day. I was excited and he actually irritated me. I thought he wanted to control me. I was always at my friend's place or surrounded by friends. Since I had the car he did not have a say as to where I wanted to go, I just did my own thing and totally ignored him. I was happy to have my car but I could not even drive properly. A month after I had my car my ex-partner damaged my car because of unfaithful reasons and he was livid, but he fixed it. I was actually doing very well financially because I was spending R8 500,00 a month on my expenses, excluding entertainment. I was saving like nobody's business on my international meal allowances and money was good in those days. I think the center of my life in 2001 was money. I wanted more money to buy bigger, better things and nobody could tell me otherwise. It was all about me and my family and friends, and ooh! I nearly forgot, and my ex-partner, in that particular order. I was selfish, come to think of it, and I wanted it all, I took my ex-partner for granted, I could not compromise and I did not want to listen to him. It was either my way or no way, it was all about me. Excitement was high and I gave my friends most of my time and completely ignored him. I was unfaithful to him and everyone wanted to be my friend because of the car. The lesson here was my car. Where is it? Where are my friends? Well, the answer is everything is lost and gone. When I look back I do not care so much about my car or my so-called friends. I lost some good loving and broke someone's heart very badly. I know now that I will choose wisely and prioritize my relationships. I must say though I was enjoying my life at that stage and I would not change it. I had the time of my life but I have learned my lessons and I have developed my character. I was not ready for any serious relationship. I was young and still wanted to have some fun and be free.

2002 Lessons:

I decided to go back home, so I broke it off with my partner. The center of my life was myself, my family and to make my mother's house a home that would rise up and greet me when I came back from work. I renovated and refurbished the house, it was my focus. I was still partying and accumulated lots of friends again, but I was starting to have accidents with my car. It was driven by everyone who wanted to and I hated to drive. I would spend a lot of money trying to fix my car with my own money because I did not have insurance. I started to fall back financially because I was paying cash for all those costly accidents while at the same time trying to maintain and refurbish my home. It was starting to get tough and it was one red flag I did not see.

2003 Lessons:

I really thought this was going to be my year but it was not. I had a major car accident in the morning on 16 May while going to work. I was doing a domestic flight, signing on at 04:45 and I had a burst tire. I went with my instinct and immediately braked, big mistake! Huge! The car flipped over and faced the opposite direction as if I were coming back from work. It was traumatic. The first person I called was my ex-partner, and he was there for me. He came and fetched me in hospital with his new lover. I called him because I knew he still had a soft spot for me, he was still in love with me and he would do anything do get back with me. He jumped whenever I needed him and was such a sweetheart, I guess my mojo was still working with him but I did not know for how long it would last. I was creating negative karma when it came to my ex- partner but I was not aware of that. I was putting myself in more debt, so I could prove to myself and my ex- partner that I could do it on my own without his help.

Keeping up appearances and drowning in debt, I was still partying with my friends. I was miserable about my car accident because I knew that it was going to cost me a lot of money. My ex-partner was helpful and supported me with advice as usual. The center of my life was my car. It was either saving money to fix it or I was going to have lots of problems with it. On 31 July I decided to phone SA prayer line in order for someone to pray for the financial problems I was facing. It started to hit then that I was starting to struggle; my spirit was always down. This was a wake-up call for me.

This was the beginning of my relationship with God. To be honest I did not know or care about God when things were going well for me. I did not even bother sometimes to thank God for all the blessings and gifts he gave me. I was in pain and I needed someone. I was starting to numb my pain by drinking a lot. It was all about my car and debts. I was stressed out, I was starting to pray more and I was always praying for a miracle. God was distant but I was still positive about everything. I was hoping and waiting for a miracle but I was still partying and clubbing, having fun and getting drunk.

On 30 August I had another car accident. I needed money desperately, I had tension headaches and my doctor said that I needed to slow down. I was sick and exhausted about my life; it was bad experiences all the way. I was asking myself, what is really happening? Why me? I did not know what to do, I did not know if I was coming or going. God was nowhere to be found. I was focusing all my energy on sorting out my debts. I was always dreaming when I was overseas that I would win a brand new car from winner's circle and a house from the Winikhaya competition. I started applying for loans. It was a rip-off but I did not care because I needed the cash desperately. This was the second red flag and God was drawing me closer to him.

2004 Lessons:

I was still Mr Motor Vehicle Accidents, always trying to fix my car or pay my debts, which were starting to accumulate. I was still recovering. I was still refurbishing my home. The center of my life was settling my debts, fixing my car and renovating my home and I was still applying for loan after loan. I was used to instant gratification; if I wanted something I wanted it now and I was not willing to wait. I was in denial about my situation and I got addicted to the loan thing, because every time when I settle one, I would get another tempting offer. I was still paying my debts on time because I wanted to build my credit score. I could not afford to pay everyone back, thank God for the meal allowance. I was starving myself overseas so that I could pay them, I was living beyond my means but I still did not get it or reduce my debts or change my lifestyle. Loans are the biggest rip-off ever. I was trying to do everything and at the same time trying to have balance. The lessons here are one thing at the time, use cash or lay-by.

2005 Lessons:

Now I was focusing on settling my car. I was putting extra cash on my installments because the last payment was due on 30 June, I was excited and pleased to settle this liability. Although my car was already ruined it was to be mine. When the day came for my last installment I started to receive calls from the bank asking me if I was going to pay the full amount or re-capitalize. I could not understand what they were saying because they talked about me paying R24 000,00. I called a friend for advice and he explained that I took the car on residual and it was either I had to trade it in for another car or pay off the settlement amount, but I could not trade it in because my car was in such an undesirable state, and one thing that frustrated me was that the sales man who sold me my car did not explain this to me and he was no longer working there. I did not qualify to buy my car but the salesman decided to sell it to me on residual so that my monthly installments would be lower without consulting me. I decided to keep the car and settle the amount by surrendering one of my investment policies at old mutual. My car was such a liability! I was starting to go crazy with my finances and my debts. Then I started to be serious about my gratitude journal. Money and having lots of it was the center of my life. I was always calculating my debts and I was shocked when I realized how much trouble I was into and still getting in. My relationship with God was getting somewhere slowly but surely, I wrote down all the things I was grateful for and I was starting to count my blessings.

All I could think about was my finances. They were stressing me out but luckily I found God in me and I love him fiercely and we were slowly getting closer. The red flags were still coming and the cracks in the wall were starting to show.

2006 Lessons:

This year I believed, hoped, and had faith that God would give me all my blessings and give me a break. I wanted God to answer all my prayers and give me the willpower to stop smoking and drinking. By the end of January I was feeling great. I had a money-making roster for February, I was full of fear and worry, not about the roster, but I had that constant feeling and I prayed to God and hoped nothing bad would happen to spoil my year. Everything was going according to plan meaning my way. I was impressed that God was actually listening to my prayers. The center of my life was having things going my way. I wanted to be the driver of my life, not knowing that God my creator is the driver of my life.

On 10 April my favorite grandmother passed on. I was relived because I knew she was suffering from a lot of pain and I could not stand seeing her suffer that way. With God's preparation I had saved a few dollars and had not changed them. They really helped me to cover the funeral. We buried her on 13 April, because we could not do it on the weekend. Everything was fully booked because it was close to the Good Friday holidays and I could not wait for the next weekend to bury her. I did not want her to stay on ice for that long and I still had a job to go to. The expense as well was going to be too much as you would imagine with black families funerals and relatives. On 1 July one of my policies matured and I decided that I was going to take all of it, not even fixing my car, to buy three tombstones for my great-grandmother, my grandmother and my aunt. On 19 August it was the unveiling of the tombstones and I was proud of myself. I was exhausted though with family politics as usual and I had to do everything by myself, with the support of my family of course. On the day of the unveiling, in the morning going to dress the tombstones, I fell asleep while driving and we nearly had an accident due to my lack of sleep because in order for everything to go smoothly I had to do almost everything by myself. It was a success and I was glad it was over, never again!

My love life came to a complete stop. I was not happy and could not understand why I was alone. I tried to prove to myself and everyone else that I could make it on my own. Damn, I was lonely. I started to hide my loneliness by drinking a lot to fill the emptiness so that I could pass out and not think. I had never been alone in my life without a partner, ever! There was always someone even if it was not serious. My patience was starting to run out, I was asking God, when? Telling God how reasonable my list was and how I deserved everything on my wish list. I thought I was getting to breaking point with my loneliness. The center of my life was my empty life, my family and my job. I wanted more because I knew that this was not what the world had to offer. I still had faith though and tried to be strong and wear one of my masks.

Patience was killing me at this point because I wanted my problems and hurt to disappear as quickly as possible but God was not answering my prayers. I asked God to help me or at least find my gifts and talents but I was still dreaming, visualizing, planning. I wanted God to just do it and make everything happen no matter what. I was pushing my way forward and it did not happen my way.

I was not in charge here, I was not the driver and I got it all wrong, God is the driver and I shall follow him always. He shall always lead me onto the right path and I shall be at the right time and place, trusting his timing because it is always perfect and impeccable. I am working on my patience and perseverance because I figure that things will never go my way, my way is not happening at all. Doing things for approval or expecting something back, keeping appearances and fishing for compliments and acceptance from people never works. I was empty and lonely, I wanted to be superman and do everything. I make myself and God first and then everybody will follow. I am starting to be a little bit selfish sometimes and take care of myself first so that I can be able to take care of others.

2007 Lessons:

I started the year hoping I was going to find a life time partner; I was frank with God and bargained with him. I started to lose my friends but I started to surrender all. I bought everyone in my family a gratitude journal. My spiritual level was climbing and my relationship with God was starting to be intimate, spiritual and philosophical. I had an amazing positive energy and attitude. The 8th May was my first official entry in my proper gratitude journal. I was excited about this venture because now at the end of each day I would consciously think and look for things that I was grateful for. My relationship with God was growing and I had people sent by God to talk to me about Jesus and baptism and I was not ready to fully commit yet, I was still searching for the perfect church.

I started to look for my second house and I wanted to do it before the national credit act was passed because I knew if I did it after I would not be able to afford it and the banks wouldn't be able to approve my second home loan. Another thing is that I wanted my space because I was feeling crowded and I wanted some peace and tranquility. I figured I wanted to start from scratch. On 24th May I applied for a home loan and I bought myself two books. They attracted me and there was so much noise about them in the media. They were about the secret and the purpose of driven life. I could not wait to read them. Everything was going my way according to me, forgetting again that nothing will go my way without God's help. I was crazy about the secret. I was always writing what I wanted to happen in my journal as if it had happened. I am sure the law of attraction works at some point but obviously the book concentrated only on the law of attraction, not mentioning other laws. Most of the things in my journal did not happen or maybe they are still manifesting in Jesus' name.

My time will come. I still relapse with quitting cigarettes no matter how much I try. I always sabotage myself by telling myself that every time I quit even if for a few days, something will stress me out so badly that I will end up relapsing because it makes me think, that is 'BS' and I know in good time I will get rid of that mentality. When the time is right, my time is my time and nobody else can take that from me.

On 26 July I started reading my first chapter about the purpose driven life. I was in Accra (Ghana). I do not know why but I wrote my obituary. I needed peace of mind because the screaming and shouting at home when I was trying to sleep from the flight or just picking my brain was driving me up the wall. This year the center of my life was all about what I wanted, my dreams, my hopes and plans. It was all about law of attraction the secret.

2008 Lessons:

Abundant life was mine, well, that is what I told myself. On 16 January I met someone and I was excited about him after a long time without anyone in my life. I was still trying to quit smoking without any success and took a break from alcohol. On 19 April I had a death on board and the experience made me realize how calm and collected I can be in stressful situations and how strong I am and I actually surprised myself. I had a very strong relationship with God. It was wonderful. I could really count on him because without him I would not have dealt with that situation so calmly. The power of God took over and I did what I could to save that old, sick man.

I eventually moved in to my new house. It was a mess but a good project to keep me busy and fired up again. It was not a smooth handover though. There was some conflict at the end because the seller did not want to move. By the end of April I was excited and could not wait to start working on my house because there was a lot of work to be done. Getting my second house was a long process and it took me a year to get everything sorted out, it was a long wait but it was worth it. I was so glad that it was finally under my name. Some of my friends thought I was lying and even suggested to me that since I was struggling and paying too much on the meter taxi, I might as well buy another car or even fix my car because it was just parked in the garage I wanted nothing to do with a car because of the realization of how much I had wasted.

I still wanted more from my Lord. I wanted to win my millions, to win my car, un-tap all of my talents and gifts. I was feeling powerful and in control, again not thinking that God gave me that power and allowed his grace to enter me. I thought the worst was over and nothing could touch me at that point. I loved the challenge of fixing my new house and the pressure that came with it.

On 22 May I was praying for the land redistribution money to come through, so that we could take care of my other grandmother who'd had a stroke. I wanted to help everyone with the money and make a difference in their lives.

By June my newfound boyfriend disappeared and I started to get lonely again. This time I was praying for God to send me my soul mate or spiritual partner. I was ready to settle down, but karma had a different idea. I had everything. I wanted God to lead me to my kind of church. By June I had started to get excited about my credit card money, I started to spend it as if it were mine, forgetting that I had to pay it back. I thought maybe God would make me a millionaire soon and I could sort them out as quickly as possible. I wanted to push everything, renovating and fixing my house, paying off my debts. I thought that could be done by October so that I could enjoy the festive season in my newly refurbished house. I was in denial and disillusioned and I thought I ran my show so well, still thinking that I was in control.

By July I was fascinated by authentic power and I made sure I looked for it everywhere and I found it in New York, the last copy, because the borders bookstore was closing down.

On 4 August my grandmother – the one who had the stroke – passed on. I was relieved and thankful because I had prayed to God to take her from all the pain and suffering and it was not easy for my mother to take care of her. She had to play her part because nobody wanted to step up and I felt sorry for her.

I wanted God to guide me and help me identify my purpose in life. My birthday was on the 08-08-2008, and I figured this must really mean something because it does not happen often. I patiently waited for something grand to happen but nothing did. I applied for a senior position at work and I was not even shortlisted for an interview. I was deeply disappointed because I wanted it so badly I could actually taste it.

My house was the center of my life. During the renovations I realized that I needed more money to finish everything and I decided again to surrender one of my policies at Old Mutual. That was the biggest the decision I had to make and I hoped I would not regret it later in my life.

On 25 September I was reading about purpose driven life again because the first time I did not get it. I was reading one chapter a day as specified by the author. I was hoping to get it this time. In early October my life was starting to slow down. Nothing major was happening and I was not happy about that because I was addicted to instant gratification. I was desperate for money and lots of it, I wanted to win something, I needed a miracle and I was also getting impatient with God, I wanted him to speed up everything just for me and unfortunately God does not work like that. There was no plan B any more, God was distant again, nowhere to be found. That did not stop me from demanding all my blessings from him. I was getting angry and agitated and I started backsliding with my relationship with God. I was more concerned now about money. By the end of October I did not have enough money to pay my second bond. I started defaulting on my credit cards payments. I did not pay on time and I hated that. I could not even buy myself decent food. I worried a lot and my fears were all coming back to me, I no longer felt powerful. I thought I was going to lose my house by just skipping one payment. I then started to gain weight because of the things I was eating.

On 01 November I tried reading about the purpose driven life again, praying to God that I would get it that every time I read it. I guess what turned me off the second time was that the book kept referring me to certain scriptures in the Bible and I was not a Bible reader. I did not even know how to read one verse because I would get so bored, let alone read different scriptures, which wasted my time because I could not even find some of them and at that time I wanted to finish whichever chapter I was reading that day, I ended up deciding to skip the Bible scriptures referred to and that is my reason for not getting it. I had to read each scripture I was referred to and understand it. So that I could move on and understand what the author was trying to tell me. I wanted direction at that point. I asked God for clues because I was really confused, I did not know where I was going. God was testing my patience because I was self-serving and self-seeking. I wanted it all and I was getting livid when the opposite happened. I was giving God my orders and bargaining with him as if I were the one in control of my life and destiny. I wanted God to serve me and be my servant, not the other way around.

On 17 November I wanted to feel God's presence. I thought God was ignoring me and by this time I was in the big pit; all my credit cards were maxed out. I started to drink and smoke heavily again and I had a lot of blackouts, which was the whole idea, I did not care as long as I did not remember but my family and friends noticed. On 16 December my life stopped but I was not giving up yet. I still had faith and trusted God that one day he would deliver all my goodies, one day! I hoped for a new day and a new beginning 2009 some kind of a fresh start. I thought God was my plan B, only to find out that he does not want to be my plan B any more – he wants to be my plan A. It dawned into me that praise from people is addictive and pleasing people is also addictive and I ended up getting lost. I do not allow people to put me on any pedestal anymore; I do what I do with the power of God.

2009 Lessons:

I wanted more love from God and I hoped he would take care of me, bless me and show me my shape so that I could serve him and others. On 08 January I started my diet and to exercise a little bit because I was getting fat. I lost the excess weight and I was also cutting on my spending overseas. That did not make any major difference; my life was still at a standstill. By stand still I mean things were not going according to plan, there were no instant gratifications, no praises, compliments or approvals. No matter how and what I tried, it was just not going anywhere. My journey was getting tougher by the day and I regretted why I had to put myself through this. I thought starting my life from scratch would be a piece of cake, I was wrong again and what made things worse was that I was starting to get calls and texts from banks and everybody that I owed. I was absolutely not used to that harassment and I did not know how to deal with the situation. Everything in my life was a mess. My US visa expired. I struggled to find anyone to lend me money for the new application, but eventually I managed to get the money. I used my meter taxi driver to take me to the Embassy by credit because I did not have enough money to use public transport. The visa did not take time to be issued, but as soon as I went to find where my driver was parked, he was not there. So I was stuck at Killarney Mall for about two hours hoping he would come back. I did not even have cash on me to go back home by public transport but I remembered that I might have at least R50,00 on one of my credit cards. Luckily I did and I managed to get back home safely, but it was a disaster.

Just when I thought the worst was over and I would be able to do my New York flight, the courier did not deliver my visa on time, so I had to lose my nice flight, which I had already budgeted for and after that the snowball effect started rolling. My nice flights disappeared because of losing that New York flight. They were calling me for not so nice flights and that affected my whole roster. I pushed myself to the limit but there was no way of moving forward. It all came back to me now and I realized that I did not have true friends, only one or two friends who are stuck with me but the rest went AWOL. It is hard for me to admit but it is the truth.

I was focusing on making money with all my energy, starving myself and working hard. I stayed in a house I could not afford, I spent all my credit as if it were mine, and my friends were gone just when I needed them the most. It was not about my roster, it was all about the love and support that I am getting from my family and I will always be grateful to God for giving me such a wonderful family.

07/May/2009- entry to my journal

There was a heavy thunderstorm when I decided to write this poem to God. I was so depressed lying in my bed alone and I got inspired by the sound of the rain and lightning. It felt as if God was comforting and reassuring me, telling me, "It's okay, my child; I can hear all your supplications and cries, I am here with you and everything will be good. Just trust in me with all your heart."

To; God be the glory

Thank you my universe finally you can see me
You can hear me
I see you outside winking at me
I hear you outside singing so loud with joy and happiness
I can hear you doing your tapping
I love you my universe
Please love me too…

Wash away all my troubles
Take away all my burdens
Lord please take them all
I give them all to you

Here is my fear
Here is my worry
Take them my lord
I give them all to you
Wash them all away

Give me all my gifts and talents

I open my heart to you now
I ask for your help my Divine Intelligence
Guide me, teach me, protect me
Let me live an abundant life that I deserve
Physically, spiritually and financially

2010 Lessons:

I had a relationship with God, and I had learned to persevere and have a little bit of patience which was tough for me. I met someone in late December 2008 I fell in love like I never had in life, I gave him my all, I loved him fiercely and I thought God had finally answered my prayers. I was wrong, I found out he was an abusive, promiscuous narcissist and a control freak who was jealous of my achievements. He wanted to alienate me from my family and friends and even attempted to kill me. He made my life miserable. He wanted me to support and work for him and ignore my needs and family responsibilities. He was just something else. He was big on using muti (traditional medicine) and consulting sangomas and that was the reason I ended up in hospital, because he wanted me to love him and only him and I guess he tried everything to tame me. My guess is they told him to use a teaspoon and he decided to use a tablespoon and that reacted badly in my lungs, because it was an overdose.

He told me of all his stories how he got arrested for hijacking, robbing and for murder at the age of sixteen. He told me he got jobs and made people love him by using muti, he told me how promiscuous he was and about his anger. I guess I thought I could change him, he was so challenging and I enjoyed that because in most of my relationships I am the one who is always in charge. Too little too late I remembered that love should not hurt and when someone tells you, "I am cruel, I am mean," believe them because they know themselves better than you know them. He treated me so badly, but I kept on believing that everything will work out eventually and we would live happily ever after. He was a cheater and a liar with a complex personality, which fascinated me sometimes. I must say I had a lot of red flags warning me in that relationship but I chose to ignore all of them. I also thought karma was involved in that situation. It all came to me at that time in vivid color. The way he treated me, the cheating, the lying (except the abusing), it was me in my younger days. I totally got it. I treated a lot of people the way he treated me. It was a taste of my own medicine and I was not proud of it. It was my turn to be on the other side and feel what it was like to be cheated on, treated and taken for granted. The taste of my own medicine was bitter! Bitter! Bitter! I do not know if I was making excuses for him and blaming myself because I know most victims of abuse are always blaming themselves but I feel my theory was right. It was supposed to happen to me and we were supposed to meet because I had a karmic debt, I was in the right place and at the right time and I do not judge. I have developed my character and I am stronger and wiser now. I have learned my lessons with that relationship and I know. I understand karma even better now; I try to be conscious of how I treat my relationship, because I do not want any comebacks.

Thank you Lord for these lessons. They were such a rollercoaster ride. I got lost and found myself. I even started consulting sangomas myself, if you cannot beat them join them; trying to find answers and trying to better my life and to speed things up because I thought God was on leave or some kind of long holiday. Everything was going so slowly. I thought, let me push it and see what is going to happen, I wanted a shortcut, a way out and I was willing to try everything and anything. After spending thousands of rands instead of paying my accounts, only to find out that there was nothing wrong with me. The sangoma told me I just needed a ceremony from my father's side so that I could be introduced to them. That opened a can of worms and secrets that my mother had been hiding from me for thirty years of my life. No wonder she was always defensive and did not want to talk or tell me about my father. I found out that the person that I thought was my father was actually not my father. My real father had passed on but luckily I knew him. He always insisted that I was his child and I wondered as a child, why did I have two fathers? It did not make sense at that time and I did not connect the dots because my mother was telling me that someone else was my father. Well, I forgave my mother; she was only fifteen going on sixteen and fragile and to find out my real father actually raped my mother was another shocker and painful to process.

It happened but all I know for sure is that I am not a mistake or an accident. You, my Lord, created me and planned me for my arrival in this universe. My lesson is: forgive! Put God first and do not rush things. I go with my heartbeat, it is me, God and the rest will follow behind. God is the driver and leader in my life, he is in total control, the only thing I must do is relax, enjoy the ride and go with God's flow. God will lead me into the right, smooth path always as long as I invite him in my life, fear him and know that he is God. He is number one in my life and anything is possible.

I found myself in hospital having operations and the Lord was with me. I cannot believe how much power he gives to me sometimes and how strong he makes me in order to deal with these circumstances in my life. I never thought I was this fragile but I realized that when God is with me, I can do all things through Christ, which strengthens me. That is why I am still here, going for year 2011. I was addicted to an abusive relationship and involved with a monster and witch but the Lord was there. I nearly ruined my life completely but thanks to God he saved me from depression, suicidal thoughts, fears, worries, negative feelings, and financial crisis. I have learned to relax and re-condition my thinking habits. A book found me, called The Power of Positive Thinking. It was awesome; I found my answers and the book directed me to the Bible. It was a wake-up call – bang! All the answers I needed were in the Bible, that is when I learned to read the Bible with an open mind because to be quite honest I always thought that the Bible was about crashing my lifestyle and sexual orientation, but it was not.

I am afraid of the Lord, I trust and believe in his word, I talk to him every chance I get and I invite God in everything I do because I know now that my Lord is so jealous about me, about guiding me and protecting me. God does not anyone, anything or any god to take credit for his work. I love the Lord and our relationship is getting stronger, still keeping the faith. So for me now God is my strength, savior, help, rock, and fortress. I totally refuse to spend my money consulting dead people who were created by God himself and making them my gods by doing unnecessary ceremonies of slaughtering animals and asking for answers they do not know. By now I would have been a millionaire; I took my last savings and made three tombstones hoping my ancestors would bless me with more money and luck but nothing happened. I did the ceremony to introduce myself to my father's side, still hoping that my circumstances and luck will change but nothing happened, instead things got worse.

I have traveled to places that I never thought I would go to and did things I thought I would never do in my life and nothing happened. The last straw was when I went to a sangoma and was told that the people for whom I had spent my last savings making the tombstones were not happy and they wanted me to slaughter a cow and two goats and two sheep's and some chickens. I said to myself it was time I gave up this ancestors thing because if they wanted all that they must make me make more money or win some jackpot. I could not even afford to buy myself chicken feet for me to eat let alone buy a live chicken to slaughter. I could not understand and actually I did not want to understand. Where were they expecting me to get money from? I do not deny the fact that sangomas and ancestors exist and work for some people but I have totally accepted that they do not work for me and I am at peace with that. They must also leave me at peace in the name of God my Jesus! I am out. I shall worship and praise only God thank you very much. I go to church and tide whatever I can and that works for me.

2011 Lessons:

I had allowed the monster in my house again to stay with me in January. Do not play Judge Judy with me, I am human and I needed to go to Boca Boca. He promised me he would never beat or lay a hand on me again and I took him back with open arms. I noticed that when everything was going wrong on his side, meaning job-wise, he came back to me. It was like he was drawing some energy or luck from me, I guess he was running low and wanted a refill somehow. By February he had gone back to his old ways. One Sunday he got a call, we were supposed to cook and spend the whole day together but he told me one of his aunts had passed on and they needed him to come to Delmas so that they could organize the funeral arrangements.

He rushed to go there and promised he would be back by the evening. There was no reason not to doubt him at that stage. I carried on with the cooking and decided to invite some of my friends over for lunch to catch up, since they were not allowed to visit or come to my house. The "cat" was away, so I had fun with my friends after a long time of not seeing them. When they left that evening and because it was getting late, I decided to call my monster and to find out if everything was okay with the funeral arrangements. Both his phones were off. I did not understand why they would be off at the same time; even if the batteries were low they cannot be off simultaneously. I had this nagging feeling and I started to go through his things. Do not get me wrong, I am not a nosy person, I respect people's privacy and I save myself from seeing things I was not meant to see. I was always given strict instructions not to touch his laptop bag, but that day the laptop bag was just calling me and I could not resist the temptation. I went for it, only to find a bunch of his contacts and a letter that he'd written to his so-called fiancé, telling him how much he wanted to marry him and loved him. I looked for his name in the contacts and I found their numbers. One of the numbers was under "Love," and I instinctively called that number without hesitation or even thinking what I was going to say when Love answered the phone. The phone rang and I was boiling inside. My heart was racing and Love finally answered his phone. I changed my voice and told him I was the monster's uncle and I just wanted to find out if the monster was with him by any chance. He said, "Hold on for him, gosh!"

I had this cold chill in my body and I think my heart stopped for a split second when the monster answered the phone in a calm and relaxed way. I asked him if this was his aunt's funeral arrangements, and he told me to stop calling him on other people's phone. "Don't follow my whereabouts, because I don't like to be traced.

"Stop calling this phone because I am so in love and I am with the person that I love and we are going to get married, I just proposed last night. Stop disturbing us because we are celebrating."

I do not know why but I was still holding the line to listen to all the hurtful stuff, he was defensive and not sorry at all. I thought to myself – never again. I will never ever put myself through this again going through people's personal things. That night I could not sleep and I drowned myself with wine waiting for the morning so that he could come back and take his belongings. All the bad things he did to me came back, he once busted my ear drum after one of our fights and I had to go and see an ear specialist to find out if there was any damage to my ears. With my career I cannot afford to lose my hearing.

This guy wanted me to lose my job so that I could suffer or finish me off for good. I was booked off for two weeks so that my ear would heal, but it was nothing serious. He brought all his boyfriends to my house while I was overseas and told them it was his house, taking photos of him and his boyfriends and showing them to my friends. He managed to come back that afternoon and he was still defensive, non-apologetic about the whole thing, he ended fighting with me for going through his things and we fought for almost the whole night. The following morning he took his belongings, my money and my house keys and locked me inside the house. I managed to get the spare keys from my sister that day and I laid a charge against him and I sought a protection order as well. This time was the last straw. I forgave him a long time ago, and I hope he gets help soon because he will end up killing someone one day. The experience taught me to develop my character even more. I thought I was strong, but he will always say when he beats me that he wanted to make me strong because I was a mommy's boy. After two court appearances I decided to drop the charges against him because I could not afford to swap or book time off work every time there was a court case. I still had the protection order against him. I truly wish him well in all his endeavors may the Lord always be with him, let him find peace, amen.

There was a big storm coming my way. On the 19 March I got sick in Munich and had lots of pain in my right side and chest. I think I was supposed to die that day in my hotel room. The pain was so excruciating, but luckily I had antibiotics that I had not used and some garlic cloves that helped me for some time, but I could not take the pain any more. I had to call one of my colleagues because I did not want to die alone in my room. It was hard making that call because I didn't want to bother people when they are relaxing in their rooms, but this was an emergency. My colleague came with my senior and they called an ambulance. I went to hospital they put me on a drip and gave me paracetamol. The doctor suggested I stay in Munich for monitoring, but I refused and insisted that I'd rather fly back home as a passenger that evening. I just wanted to go home and get sick around the people I love because it is not nice to get sick out of the country. The doctor discharged me and diagnosed with pulmonary pneumonia. I went back to the hotel that same night, it was better and I think the drip worked for some time, I think I needed something stronger for the pain than paracetamol. Late that evening the pain got stronger and stronger and the trip to the airport felt like the longest ever bus trip, I could not sit still in the bus because it made the pain even worse. For the entire flight I was on oxygen. I think I finished seven oxygen bottles; I could not sleep or eat on that flight, it was also the longest flight I have ever done. On the flight I could not stop blaming myself, thinking

I should have ordered a room service instead of venturing in the freezing snowing cold. On 20 March I was at home and got admitted to the Glynnwood hospital. My doctor mismanaged me, and failed to do more tests to find out exactly what was wrong with me. The last test he did was an ultrasound, and it showed that I had a small right-sided pleural effusion, which means liquid in my lung. It was getting larger but he opted to discharge me on 29 March.

On 7 April I went to work for a check-up so that I could be cleared to go back flying. The Doctor at the medical department noted some consolidation build-up in my right lower middle lung regions and insisted I had X-rays. When the results came back they confirmed that I could not go back flying until the fluid in my lung had been properly drained. Thank God I work for such a company, because I would have carried this around without knowing it was getting larger – and God knows what it would have done to my lung.

On the 10 April the pain returned and I was admitted to ARWYP hospital. My doctor diagnosed me of atypical pneumonia, which was just an assumption because there had been no bacteria found in all the tests that he had done. When I asked him what was wrong with me he kept on saying it was an infection; he just did not know what was wrong with me, nobody knew. On 11th April another doctor did a lung biopsy – he could not do anything but he also kept on telling me it was an infection. My diagnosis was unknown here as well, and I was also mismanaged and under-treated. ARWYP was the biggest private hospital in Africa, with enough facilities for the doctors to do more tests.

The day after that I had the draining pipes removed. I collapsed trying to take my bath, and my doctor was not available to attend to me. It was all a guessing game. My collapse caused me to have seizures later that afternoon at 4.30pm for forty-five seconds, and another one at 5.20pm for two minutes. Then I was transferred to ICU and handcuffed to my bed. It was such a painful situation not being able to move freely. The hospital staff only did this because I was kicking and beating the nurses. When I think about that traumatic moment, tears run in my eyes, it was like I lost my mind I could not understand if I was turning blind or dying. All I know in that moment is that I fought my toughest battle – and that is why I am still alive today.

I was actually was supposed to die that afternoon. Thank God for giving me the strength to fight that battle. The seizures would have been avoided if there was a doctor attending me. It is on the 17 April that the doctor who was treating me for seizures made an appearance, and when I asked what was causing the seizures, she told me it was meningitis, caused by an infection and I was then later discharged on 24 April and booked off until 31 May 2012.

On 1 June I went back to work on ground duties because I was still medically unfit. The Civil Aviation Authority (CAA) wanted full medical reports from all my Doctors to be submitted to them so that they could review my case before I went back on flying duties. Working on the ground was frustrating and it was such a struggle not being able to move around freely. I had to really dig in and push myself. It was the first time in my life doing office work and it was not easy for me to adjust to an environment full of politics.

The first report was ready for collection from the Doctor who treated me when I was first admitted to ARWYP. I went to his offices and he gave me the report for me to read. He wrote that I had developed convulsions while hospitalized. I was not happy about that part because I know that as the flight attendant your flying career was over if you had unexplained convulsions. I begged him to remove that part but he refused, saying he did not want any comebacks or to lose his license. Now I had to really think hard about whether to submit this report or not. While I was at work I decided that day to check my roster, only to find out that I was rostered for July, I thought to myself, I was going to do those flights. I was broke, I needed the money. On 1 July I did a domestic flight just to test the water, to find out if they would take notice. They did not and I carried on doing my rostered flights as if it was normal. On 19 July the medical department needed me to do a lung function test. They tried to locate where I was working on the ground with no success until they checked my roster only to find out I was in Washington! It was time to face the music. In the morning while I was sleeping in Washington I received a call from my manager. I knew the instant that I heard his voice that they had caught my illegal flying business. He told me that he had booked me as a passenger for the flight leaving that afternoon to Johannesburg. I was panicking, scared and kicking myself. I thought, this is it, I have lost my job for a couple of dollars. I landed at the airport thinking my manager would be waiting at the aircraft door. I stayed a week before I gathered enough courage to face them. I consulted my union and told them the story. Luckily they found a loophole and I was just given a verbal warning, thank God for that. Now I had no choice but to submit the first report and they told me if I could get the report from the Doctor who treated me for the seizure explaining what caused the convulsions I would be good to go. My Doctor wrote that I had meningitis and I had seizures due to infection and that opened another can of worms. CAA wanted more details regarding the duration of my seizures; how far apart where they? Was the diagnosis of meningitis confirmed and how?

Was there any other explanation for the seizures? Did I have increased risks of sudden or subtle incapacitation? I had to pay for my medical file to be released in order for my Doctor to know how far apart the seizures were. It was such a mission but eventually I managed to get it. My Doctor responded to all their questions in her medical report and stated again that I had no risk of sudden incapacitation and it was safe for me to perform my flying duties. CAA had more questions for her. They wanted to know, was the lumbar puncture done or was it contraindicated? What confirmatory tests were done? What kind of meningitis had I had? And what treatment was given for it? After my Doctor received these questions I immediately got a call from her secretary telling me that my Doctor would not be writing anymore medical reports and I must just sue CAA because there is no reason for them not clear me to perform my flying duties. I told this to the Doctor at CAA who was presenting my case and he told me that I must complain about my Doctor at Health Profession Council of South Africa(HPCSA), I did lay a written detailed complaint hoping that would push my Doctor to explain and give more clarity on my case. I also complained about my initial Doctor and also the one who treated me in Glynwood. I thought to myself, why would my Doctor not want to explain? Unless she had something to hide? It made sense to complain about her and others because of all the mismanagement, and under-treatment I had received from Glynwood hospital.

This grounding was affecting my life immensely. I stayed for two months and took unpaid leave because I was struggling to go to work. This Doctor was putting my life at a complete standstill. I also felt that my case at CAA was dealt with unfairly because they did not allow me to get a second opinion from another independent neurologist to find out if I was prone to having other seizures or if I had epilepsy. Their decision to declare me unfit was rushed. The umbrella of this whole case was the meningitis because my Doctor did not do a lumbar puncture and also they thought that I had epilepsy. My flying career was over but I still had hope that after six months of taking anti-convulsion medication they would consider my case but CAA said that without any new reports from the Doctor there was no chance for me at the panel. The HPCSA case was also just taking forever. Depression was knocking on my door. I was unable to pay for anything with the salary I was getting on the ground. It was getting worse by the day. I was asking myself, who am I? What is it that I am supposed to do here on earth school?

2012 Lessons:

Perseverance and Patience

It had been more than a year, fighting to go back to my flying duties but every effort I made was getting me nowhere. This year was the worst ever. My cup was overflowing. I was tired of fighting and sometimes I would stay at home for months without going to work. That was unpaid leave. I was at a point where I just did not give a continental. I hated being on the ground; waking up every morning was a struggle. Nothing motivated me to wake up and go to work, it was just not me. I thought it was too much for me, I thought I could not handle it. I got a letter from the bank informing me that they were auctioning off my house since I had not paid the agreement I had made with them. My mother was admitted to hospital, my sister was spinning out of control with drugs and unprotected sex. I nearly became an alcoholic. I was a clown behind the glass, everyone was clearing the way for my crash landing because I drank, not just for fun anymore but to numb my pain to a point where I would have blackouts, which were fantastic at that time. I was fighting with the medical department, CAA, HPCSA, and managers at work. They were making a lot of noise because they were implementing the incapacity policy and wanted all grounded flight attendants to do training and go work at the airport. I ended up going to see a psychologist and a psychiatrist just to get evaluated as to whether I was losing it or not or if I was at risk of killing myself, only to find out it was just normal anxiety and depression and I did not need to take medication, thank God for that.

I would go for months without food at work and just declare it as my fasting. It was a tough journey that taught me to be patient and know that perseverance is the mother of success. That made me realize that you can fast for the whole year but if it is not yet your time it won't happen because God's timing is perfect. I now can proudly say that I know how to stand still and I am able to pick myself up no matter what comes my way, with the grace of God. With all these circumstances I told myself I would not take any shortcuts this time. I told myself that I would not backslide this time. I stood firm but I must say it was not easy. I grew the most when I entered the zone of the unknown but God was with me all the time very quiet and not doing anything but watching my reactions. That is when I knew that I still had it; I was still growing, developing and expanding my character.

I too have walked this path my friend, I too have felt the pain you have felt. Yet I have learned that everything happens for a reason. Every event has a purpose and every setback has its lesson. I have realized that failure, whether personal, professional or even spiritual, is essential to personal expansion. It brings inner growth and a whole host of psychic rewards. As long as I live I will never regret my past lessons, mistakes, circumstances, trials and tribulations. I will always embrace them as the teachers they are. I even applied for a position where I was working at the ground because I thought I would never go back to flying. The position already had someone's name on it and they were just covering up by interviewing us and honestly that was upsetting. I also did not get the senior position I applied for at in-flight. I may not have gone where I intended to go but I ended up where I was intended to be by the grace of God.

I had to empty my cup. It was full of my own ideas about life and no more could get in. Investing in myself was the best investment I ever made; it improved my life and those around me. I have learned that self mastery and consistently taking care of myself, mind, body and soul are essential to finding my highest self and living the life of my dreams. I take good care of myself first so that I can care for others. I feel good so that I can do good and I love myself more so that I can love others. This was what was emphasized by the psychologist and the psychiatrist.

Looking back now, all that happened for a fantastic reason. I made good friends when I had no friends to count on. They were with me, supporting me all the way. I had a very caring manager and I loved her. She was such a mother she made me do all the computer courses and was supportive of my venture into furthering my education. If I was still flying I would still be singing the same song of registering but because I was on the ground I had the time to apply for a bursary and get it and with all the circumstances I passed all four subjects, one with distinction. My brother found a job and everything is looking great for 2013. Hallelujah!

Chapter 11

Evolution

I am evolving and I am an evolver. As a human being I am a member of the most complex species and therefore the most evolved life-forms upon our planet. I am at the top of the food chain. Jesus was one of the most evolved of our species because he valued others more than he valued himself and he valued love more than he valued the physical world and what was in it. I have evolved to now and I am in the process of leaving behind this phase of evolution. I must now bring my understanding of evolution into alignment with the new and expanded understanding of evolution, one that validates my deepest truths, so that I can see what I am evolving into and what that means in terms of what I experience, what I value and how I act.

I have been until now a five sensory human being, I stopped chasing external power and left it behind. My mission now is to chase authentic power, a power that loves life in every form that it appears in, a power that does not judge what it encounters, a power that perceives meaningfulness and purpose in the smallest details upon earth. This happens when I align my thoughts, emotions and actions with the highest part of myself. It is when I am filled with enthusiasm, purpose and meaning, when life is rich and full, when I have no thoughts of bitterness, no memory of fear, when I am joyously and intimately engaged with my world. This is the experience of authentic power. I am on a journey toward authentic power and that authentic empowerment is the goal of my evolutionary process and the purpose of my being. I am evolving from a species that pursues authentic power. I am evolving from five-sensory human into multi-sensory human. I am never alone; my universe is alive, conscious, intelligent and compassionate. I must align my personality with my soul because I was not always meant to be five sensory. I must understand evolution that five sensory leads to multi sensory.

Karma

I am now aware of my immortal soul. The lifetime of my personality is one of a vast number of experiences of my soul. My soul exists outside of time and it has incarnated its energies many times into many psychological and physical forms. For each incarnation my soul creates a different personality and body. My personality contributes in its own special way, with its own special aptitudes and lessons to learn consciously or unconsciously to the evolution of my soul. My life as a bread winner and firstborn son, my experiences of love, responsibility, fear, loss and tenderness, my struggle with patience, loneliness and pride, they all serve the evolution of my soul.

Each physical, emotional and psychological trait that comprises my personality and my body is perfectly suited to my soul's purpose but my personality and my body are artificial aspects of my soul because when they have served their functions my soul release them. They come to an end but my soul does not. I am here again on earth school because some parts of my soul require healing. I need to become whole. I now take responsibility for all my actions. I receive from the world what I give to the world that is karma for me. I am the change that I want to see. Everyone in this world, has karmic debts so I cannot judge what I see as unfair because I do not know what is being completed and healed for that soul.

There is a lot of negativity here on earth. I see it every day but I cannot judge it because it is not my place and when I judge I create negative karma for myself. This does not mean that I should not act appropriately in the circumstances in which I find myself. I should not act superior to another person even if they are in the wrong because that will increase the karmic obligations of my soul. Negative karma must be balanced and is necessary. That is why there are all these sufferings in the world. I try not to judge and have a non-judgmental justice, which means I must see everything in life but I must not engage my negative emotions because everything is being seen and nothing escapes the law of karma. I must have the freedom of seeing what I see and experiencing what I experience without responding negatively. This reminds me of my current situation and now I understand my situation even better. I could not understand and I was a self-appointed judge when people said, "I have five credit cards and now they are all maxed out and I am unable to pay for them". I would judge those people and ask myself, how would a person do that to themselves? I did not understand why. Why do people spend money that they do not have? Do they know that they have to pay it back? Even worse, with interest.

I used to have this frustration and anger with a passion, acting as if I knew better and feeling superior. I did not know what was being completed and healed for those souls. I did not understand. I continued my judging. Now I know better that my crisis was a test and a karmic debt. I am extra careful now because every time I say I do not understand something or do not understand a situation I end up being in that situation. I allowed myself to judge these events and those who participated in them. I created negative karma for myself, which must be balanced. From now on no judging for me, I will leave that for Judge Judy thank you very much.

Reverence

I became reverent and reverence is simply the experience of accepting that all life is, in and of itself of value. Life is not cheap and it does not matter if that life is for an animal, a person or a plant, everything matters in this universe. I always thought that this world was a dog-eat-dog world and that to survive in it I must take advantage of others before they took advantage of me. I looked at life as a contest that produces winners and losers. I thought it was the design of nature; it was survival of the fittest for me. I am on top of the food chain and I concluded that weaker forms of life exist only to nourish the stronger. My perceptions lacked reference. I was arrogant; I behaved as though the earth was mine to do as I pleased with not even thinking of the needs of other life forms that lived upon the earth or of the needs of the earth.

Now I have the attitude of honoring every form of life and harming nothing. I look at what I am going through and see it within the framework of the evolution and maturation of my own spirit that enables me to look at all the evolutions that are taking place simultaneously with my own, in all the kingdom of life and fully appreciate or at least see very differently how they unfold. Every living creature has a significance or a role to play in this universe. I work towards becoming reverent and my tendencies toward harming others and other forms of life diminish. I think more deeply about the value of life before I commit my energy to action.

Reverence automatically brings forth patience and permits non-judgmental justice. Without reverence my experiences are brutal and destructive but with my experiences become compassionate and caring. I have come to honor all of life, all that happens and the quality of experiences that I will have as I learn. The time has come for a higher order of logic and understanding that is capable of meaningfully reflecting the soul and that comes from the heart. I pay close attention to my feelings and being aware of them so that I can experience compassion. I am intimate with my emotions because my emotions reflect my intentions; therefore awareness of my emotions leads to awareness of my intentions. Without awareness of my emotions I will not be able to experience reverence. Reverence is not an emotion, it is a way of being but the path to reverence is through my heart and only an awareness of my feelings can open my heart. I live my life in light and stay away from evil because evil is the absence of light and love in all cases. I understand evil for what it is and never fight it, run from it or outlaw it. Every time evil approaches me I just move to the light and conscious light is equal to divinity, that is my Divine Intelligence, God. Where there is an absence of God, darkness moves in. The existence of darkness is not permanent; my soul will eventually be fully enlightened because there is so much assistance provided all the time.

The encouragement to take even one thought into light is always available; understanding that evil is the absence of light does not mean that it is inappropriate to respond to evil. The remedy for an absence is the presence of God. By hating evil or one who engages in evil acts, you contribute to the absence of light and not to its presence. Hatred of evil does not diminish evil; it increases it. When I hate I bring that suffering upon myself. I try to be compassionate to those who commit evil acts because if I strike without compassion against the darkness, I myself enter the darkness.

By having a compassionate heart I can engage evil directly, I can bring light where there was no light. From now on I examine the choices I make, each moment in terms of whether it moves me toward light or away from it. This allows me to look with compassion upon those who engage in evil activities even as I challenge their activities. I am able to protect myself from creating negative karma. It permits me to see that the place to begin the task of eliminating evil is within myself; this is an appropriate response to evil. The next phase of my evolution is taking me into the experiences of the multi sensory human and the nature of authentic power. This requires the heart.

Chapter 12

I am not alone in this universe and I do not need to rely only on my own perceptions and interpretations of events for guidance because I am in conscious communication with other more advanced intelligences. This means that I have conscious access to compassionate and impersonal help in the analysis of my choices, their probable consequences and in the exploration of different parts of myself. With all the help and guidance that is available to me I understand more quickly now the meaning of my experiences, how they come into being, what they represent and my role in creating them. Now I do not need to experience two hundred painful experiences in order to learn my major lesson.

I am wiser now and I am full of compassion. There are always sources of guidance and assistance that surround me and they are always available to me. I am talking about my insight, my intuitions, my hunches, my gut feelings and my inspirations. These are all messages from the soul or from advanced intelligences that assist the soul on its evolutionary journey. I have learned to increase my awareness of these guidance's and incorporate them consciously into my life. The first step to this is becoming aware of what I am feeling and following my feelings, which leads me to their source. Every question that I ask is always answered and every time I ask for guidance and help I receive it.

Sometimes I do not hear the answers to my questions when I ask them and the answers always come in ways I do not expect but they always come. The answers comes in forms of a feeling, a "yes" feeling or a "no" feeling, sometimes in the form of a memory or a thought that at that time seems random, sometimes in a dream and sometimes in the form of realization that is prompted by an experience that will occur the next day. I am in the process of learning to develop and employ my intuition. I have learned to ask for help and guidance and how to receive it. I think the first step to engaging and disciplining my intuition is to honor emotional cleansing at all times. I must keep my emotions clear of any emotional negativity and this will open my intuitive track because it will allow me to have a clear sense of loving. It will bring me closer to unconditional love and lightens the quality of my frequency so to speak and therefore the guidance that I will receive will be clear and unobstructed as it enters my system. I must dispose of all my emotional waste and toxins everyday by finishing emotionally unfinished business and not going to bed angry.

The second step is a cleansing nutritional program and fasting. I try to exercise and eat healthy food that is highly beneficial to my blood type because being physically toxic interferes with intuition. The third step is to honor the guidance that I receive. Emotional and physical cleansing leads to intuition and this leads to learning to respond. I am willing to hear what my intuition says and act accordingly. The fourth step is to allow myself an orientation of openness toward my life with a sense of faith and trust that there is a reason for everything that is happening and that reason at its heart is always compassionate and good. This is an essential thought that needs to be in place in order to activate and cultivate intuition.

My intuition is meant to assist me and serves many purposes in my life. It serves my survival, my creativity and my inspiration. The experience of intuition cannot be explained in terms of the five senses because it is the voice of the non physical world; therefore it is not possible to understand my soul or my higher self or my intuition without coming to terms with the existence of non-physical reality. I am a system of light as are all beings, the frequency of my light depends upon my consciousness. When I shift the level of my consciousness, I shift the frequency of my light. If I choose to forgive someone who has wronged me for example, rather than to hate that person, I shift the frequency of my light. If I choose to feel affection for a person rather than distance or coldness I shift the frequency of my light.

Emotions are currents of energy with different frequencies. Emotions that I think of as negative, such as hatred, envy and fear have a lower frequency and less energy than emotions that I think of as positive, such as affection, joy, love and compassion. When I choose to replace a lower frequency current energy such as anger with a higher frequency energy such as forgiveness, I raise the frequency of my light. When I choose to allow higher frequency currents of energy to run through my system I experience more energy. Different thoughts create different emotions. Thoughts of vengeance, violence and greed or thoughts of using others for example, create emotions such as anger, hatred, jealousy and fear. These are low frequency currents of energy and they lower the frequency of my light or consciousness.

Creative, loving, or caring thoughts invoke high frequency emotions such as appreciation, forgiveness and joy; they raise the frequency of my system. If my thoughts are thoughts that draw low frequency energy currents to me, my physical and emotional attitudes will deteriorate and emotional or physical disease will follow, whereas thoughts that draw high frequency energy currents to me create physical and emotional health. By choosing my thoughts and by selecting which emotional currents I release and which I reinforce I determine the quality of my light.

Light represents consciousness. When I do not understand something I say, I bring it to light. If I am confused, I say I need more light. When I finally get it I say that the light has come on or I call it an "AHA" moment. When I release a negative thought or negative feeling I increase the frequency of my consciousness. My soul has both guides and teachers and they assist my soul in every phase of its evolution. My soul knows its guides and teachers, it draws upon their wisdom and compassion. I always receive loving guidance and assistance at each moment, at each moment I am prompted and encouraged to move into light.

The decisions I make are mine to make. A non-physical teacher cannot and would not live my life for me. It will assist me through the learning experiences of my life; the answers that it can provide will depend upon the questions I ask. I ask direct questions about my own motivations. I pray and meditate and am always open for answers because when I ask one set of questions, one set of doorways opens before me and when I ask other questions, other doorways open.

In each instance my teachers will advise me with impersonal compassion and clarity. My guides and teachers help me examine the probable results of each choice that I make. My teachers touch my feelings in ways that bring my awareness to areas that need to be healed. My teachers answer my questions but I must ask them and therefore give direction to my own energy. My teachers advise me as to which courses will most likely lead to which result and they continue to advise me with wisdom and compassion, no matter what choice I make. A teacher can neither create nor remove karma for me. No one, not even my non-physical teacher can assume responsibility for my life, for the way that I choose to use my energy but my teachers can help me understand what my choices and my experiences represent. My guides and teachers provide me with knowledge that allows me to choose responsibly and hopefully choose wisely. Every decision I make either moves me toward my personality or toward my soul. Each decision I make is an answer to my question. I have learned through wisdom and not through doubt and fear.

I am a dynamic being of light that at each moment informs the energy that flows through me. I do this with each thought and with each intention. The light that flows through my system is universal energy; it is the light of the universe. I give that light form by what I feel, think, how I behave, what I value and how I live my life. This reflects the way that I shape the light that flows through me. I must change the way shape my light by changing my consciousness. I must be more aware of my thoughts, feelings and actions. I must challenge negative patterns such as anger and consciously choose to replace them with compassion. I must challenge my impatience and consciously choose to understand and appreciate the needs of others. By doing this I will create different forms of thought, feelings and actions. This will change my experiences hugely.

I must intend to change my experience and use my willpower because I create my reality with my intentions and my intentions shape my light. I am the product of the karma of my soul. The dispositions, aptitudes and attitudes I was born to serve the learning of my soul. Now I realize that anger leads to nowhere. My anger disappeared and I moved into a more integrated and mature orientation toward my experiences. What once angered me now brings forth different responses. I am aware of the effects of my anger and I am no longer an angry person. My intentions create the reality that I experience; I am mindful of what I project, which is the first step toward my authentic power.

Every intention sets energy into motion, whether I am aware of it or not. I create in every moment; each word that I speak carries consciousness more than it carries intelligence and therefore is an intention that shapes light. I cannot become compassionate with myself without becoming compassionate with others or vice versa. When I am compassionate with myself and others my world becomes compassionate. I draw to myself other souls of like frequency and with them I create, through my intention and my actions and my interactions, a compassionate world. As I come to seek and see the virtues and strengths and nobilities of others I begin to seek and see them in myself also.

As I draw to myself the highest frequency currents of each situation, I radiate that frequency of consciousness and change the situation. I become more and more consciously a being of light. To become aware of the relationship between my consciousness and physical reality is to become aware of the law of karma, to see it in action. What I intend is what I become, my challenge is creation, I always create with reverence. The center of the evolutionary process is choice and it is the engine of my evolution. I make responsible choices because that is the conscious road to my authentic power. I choose consciously where and how I will focus my energy since I have different parts of myself that need to be satisfied.

Only through responsible choice can I choose consciously to cultivate and nourish the needs of my soul and to challenge and release the wants of my personality. This is the choice of clarity and wisdom, the choice of conscious transformation. It is the choice to follow the voice of my higher self, my soul. It is the decision to open myself to the guidance and assistance of my guides and teachers, it is the path that leads consciously to authentic power. My struggles themselves do not create karma or determine the way I will evolve, only my responses to them do. I choose consciously how I respond in order to create the karma I desire. I am constantly receiving guidance and assistance from my guides and teachers and from the universe itself which is God.

If I choose consciously to move toward the energy of my soul, I invite that guidance when I ask the universe to bless me in my effort to align myself with my soul. I open a passageway between myself and my guides and teachers. I assist their efforts to assist me and I invoke the power of the non-physical world. I am also aware of the temptations and wants of my personality and needs of my soul and I try to align myself with the energy of my soul and empower myself so that I can acquire authentic power. I challenge all the negative feelings in my life so that I can gain my power back.

Chapter 13

I have an addictive personality. I get so easily addicted, mostly to bad habits and sometimes I just cannot beat temptation. I easily give myself permission to be irresponsible and I am learning to say no to myself because I love myself fiercely now. The desires and impulses that I often feel are irresistible; I lack the power to overcome my addictions. My addictions are the wants of the parts of my personality that are very strong and resistant to the energy of my soul. They are those aspects of my personality that are most in need of healing. They are my greatest inadequacies, my holes that I need to always fill up but funnily enough they are never full.

I am so insecure that no matter how hard I try to defeat my addictions I feel as if I just cannot survive without them. I feel incomplete and empty without my addictions, I am powerless without them. Now I am experiencing the causes and effects of my choices. I would always have the desire to fill on the empty holes and powerless places within me. Depending on the glasses I wear to interpret my crisis I either step closer to my soul or closer to the earth. My journey to wholeness requires that I look honestly, openly and with courage into myself, into the dynamics that lie behind what I feel, what I perceive, what I value and how I act. It is a journey through my defenses and beyond, so that I can experience consciously the nature of my personality and face what it has produced in my life and choose to change that.

I acknowledge my addictions and one that bothers me is smoking. I know it is not good for my health but I keep on relapsing. I always rationalize it and make it desirable or attractive, sometimes even beneficial because I always maintain my weight when I smoke. This is one of the places where I lose power in my life and where I am controlled by external circumstances. My smoking addiction is out of control and my personality resists acknowledging this addiction because it means I have to change my whole life and my self-image. I have the fear, what would be I without a fag? I get so miserable my body aches in pain. I feel as if the is this magnet that pulls me back whenever I try to quit. I must enter my own fear and try to truly realize that what stands between me and a different life is a matter of responsible choices.

I must use my power to make responsible choices to empower myself so that I can be whole, walk myself through my own reality step by step, making myself aware of consequences of my decisions and choose accordingly. When I feel the cravings of my addictions I must remember to ask myself these questions: By following those impulses do I increase my level of enlightenment? Does it bring me enlightenment of the genuine sort? Will it make me more whole? Will I gain something from it? Now I know that I stand between the two worlds of my lesser self and my full self. my lesser self is tempting and powerful because it is not as responsible and not as loving or as disciplined, so it calls me. The other part of me is whole and more responsible and more caring and empowered but it demands me to choose the way of enlightenment and conscious life.

The power is fully in my hands, it is really up to me. I must not underestimate the power of consciousness. As I live my life and make conscious choices, each moment of each day I am filled with strength and my lesser self disappears. I choose to empower myself by challenging my addictions and temptations. I know by doing that they will surface again and again but I also know that each time I challenge them I will gain power and they will lose power. I must look upon each recurrence as an opportunity that is offered to me. In response to my intention, to release my inadequacy and to acquire power over it, I will hold on to my intention to quit smoking and will choose again and again to eventually become whole. By doing that I will accumulate power and the addiction that I think cannot be challenged will lose its power over me.

I am reaching for healing and taking this journey toward wholeness. It is not easy but I know that assistance is always there for me from my guides and teachers. I am consciously shifting upward into higher frequencies of light. In order to release my addictions it is necessary for me to enter my inadequacies, to recognize that they are real and I must bring them into the light of consciousness to heal. It is essential for me to look deeply into parts of myself that have such power over me and look clearly at how deep they are within me and to see them as honestly as I can.

I must say though that my addiction to smoking has provided me with one of the few genuine pleasures in my stressful life but what is more important to me now is my wholeness and my freedom and not the pleasure that I get from satisfying my addictions. I must understand that my addictions are results of my inadequacies. The question is how will I respond to my inadequacies? This is going to be a very painful process because I must move into how strong the power of my addiction is, into how deeply I feel its attraction and ask myself if the time is really right for me to release this form of learning. Am I strong enough to change my way of living my life? I must take the path of higher wisdom that my guides and teachers are offering me. I must be honest. I struggle with and fear my addiction and sometimes I doubt my power to challenge it successfully but at least I keep on trying again and again.

I am dealing directly with the healing of my soul and with the matter of my life. This is the work that I am required to do. I will reach my highest goal by facing my deepest struggles. As I bring to light, heal and release the deepest currents of negativity within me, I allow the energy of my soul to move directly into and shape the experiences and events of physical reality. This is the work of evolution and it is the work that I was born to do.

One thing I am not good at is maintaining my relationships. I am just going round and round in circles and sometimes I even blame myself. I get bored quickly and I want everything to be about me and revolve around me. I need to be in a committed relationship with someone so that I can learn to care for them more than myself. I need to learn to value the growth of strength and clarity in another soul, even if that threatens the wants of my personality. I need to release the wants of my personality in order to accommodate and encourage someone else's growth. I must find my spiritual partner so that we can take this journey together toward authentic power but first I must change the way I do things because if I do not I will keep getting the same results.

By committing myself to a spiritual partnership I will begin to form and live by the values, perceptions and actions that reflect equality with my partner and a commitment to their spiritual development and my own. I must set aside the wants of my personality in order to accommodate the needs of my partner's spiritual growth and in doing so will grow myself. I must see that what is necessary to the health of my partnership is identical to what is necessary to my own spiritual growth.

I must value my partner's contribution to my development and experience their helpful perceptions and observations. I must learn the roles of love, commitment and trust, give my all so that I can make it work. I must learn that love alone is not enough, that without trust I will not be able to give and receive the love that both of us have for each other. I must learn that our commitment must be translated into a form that satisfies the needs of both of us. I must value the needs of my partner as much as I value my own because the partnership that we both want requires two healthy and secure individuals. I must learn to trust not my partner, but also our ability to grow together and lastly always be truthful and have no secrets, leave all my fears and doubts and enter into the commitment with full force.

My temptation becomes greater when I am in a relationship as does my ability to make responsible choices, but I will shine brighter because my light and power increase with every responsible choice. I am wiser now and this time I want it all! I am empowered now and I know I can change my destiny, although one psychic told me that I am not lucky in relationships, I choose not to believe that hogwash and I am going to change all that, change my energies and stop being so selfish and start to be patient with my partner. It is not about me; sometimes though I console myself that the only commitment I have here on earth, when it comes to relationships is my family. This is the only relationship I can maintain but I guess they do not have a choice but to love me. They are the only people who can tolerate my bullshit. Another thing with me is that when it comes to love affairs I have these walls that protect me but I guess I was living my life in fear and doubt because of my past experiences with love. Now I choose to live my life with wisdom and reverence. My intentions were good in all my past relationships but when things started going wrong, I was the first one to call it quits. I was weak when it came to temptation; I was the one who was always unfaithful. Now is the time to change and make responsible choices.

Chapter 14

I have an individual soul in this earth school and there is more than one avenue from which individual souls are formed. My soul has chosen to move through kingdom evolution, it chose this planet to have human experiences so that it can heal and balance its energy and also pay its karmic debts. What I like about this universe is that I am not alone. I have different souls always around me, souls that chose to learn by becoming my non-physical guides and teachers, my angels. To me this brings more understanding to the issue of my ancestors. My non-physical guides and teachers are the souls of my ancestors. For some time I believed this theory but I am not so sure about it now but I am still grateful to have angels around me all the time, whoever they are. It is such a relief to know that they choose to protect me. All I know is that my angels are no longer human, therefore it is not appropriate for me to consider them from the dynamic of the personal. It is more appropriate for me to think of them as an impersonal consciousness. They are spirits and they have whole souls so they cannot be understood in human terms. They are the teachers of my life and they are free to teach me in my life without being in my life. I am existing in duality and my angels are not but I am destined to evolve beyond the nature of duality. Eventually everything will make sense. When I leave my physical form I will join the non-physical level of reality that is appropriate to my vibration frequency at that time I leave my incarnation.

I am an old soul and I wonder though, why do I keep coming back? Why does my soul keep re-incarnating? What is it that I have to heal to make my soul whole? What energy do I have to balance? What karmic debts do I have to pay? I do not know the answers yet but I think I have got some idea. It is going to be a journey but eventually I will get there, step by step. It is actually going to be easier now since I know that my guides and teachers will be there to guide and teach me in every decisions that I make. I believe in God even more now but I used to also believe in sangomas and psychics. Now I know better, that God does not want competition. My God is jealous and does not want to share me. I also know that there are legitimate people here on earth who have the power to communicate with the non physical world. This is a range of human beings with numerous frequencies and qualities of consciousness, many of whom guide and help us interact with our non physical guides and teachers. There are angels around me and they have a level of sight and knowledge that prevents certain things or actions from happening in my life. Paranormal activities are real, they come from those souls who do not pursue the journey back to their higher selves but remain bound with their non-physical individual states close to the earth school. They are negative spirits, ghosts or possessions. They always encourage negativity and are drawn to people who are weak and full of negative thoughts. In this case I am so glad that they won't come near me, I am sure they have tried their luck but have failed because I am full of positive thoughts and energy and I always monitor my thoughts consciously. This all means that there are numerous souls and spirits of non physical life and it is a reality that we must all face and be aware of.

My soul has no beginning and no end. My soul is powerful and I must turn my attention to the needs of my soul. I must consider what is required by my soul in order to be healthy. I must help my soul to attain what is necessary to its evolution and its health. My body is the instrument of my soul and I must always honor my soul. My body needs rests and care but behind every aspect of health or illness of my body is energy of my soul. It is the true purpose of the human experience and everything serves that. I must understand what my soul can tolerate and what contributes to its health and what breaks its health down.

I must understand how my behaviors and activities affect my soul. I must not create more negative karma for my soul because now I truly understand that the experiences of my life are necessary to the balancing of the energy of my soul. From now on I will not react to them personally. As I am a multi-sensory personality, I must acquire knowledge through my intuition and process that knowledge step by step to align my soul with my personality because the conscious path to authentic power requires recognition of the non-physical dimensions of my being, of my soul and the growing knowledge of what my soul is and what it wants. My spirituality encompasses my whole soul's journey, whereas my intuition is the way that my soul can contact my beingness to help it to survive situations or in creative situations or in inspirational situations. It is the way; through my higher self I can ask and receive assistance from other souls and from my teachers and guides.

I am now fully aware of the guidance from my higher self and I am receptive to it and that receptivity allows guidance to flow instantly and immediately. I must say though that it took me a while because I was so unaware and denied that there was any level of higher wisdom and guidance to my life, I had to go through major crisis, pain and suffering because then the guidance came through the density of physical events. I am again being given the chance to choose how I will learn and how will I evolve. This is a time for me as an individual to choose again. It is an opportunity for me to choose otherwise, to choose this time to learn love through wisdom, to take the vertical path of clarity, of conscious growth and conscious life.

The illusion of my soul is created by my intentions and the illusion is alive at each moment with the most appropriate experiences that I can have in order for my soul to heal. When I experience fear, anger or jealousy, I am in an illusion that is designed to bring awareness to those parts of the soul that require healing. These things do not actually exist, that is why pursuing them does not bring power. The illusion holds power over me when I am unable to remember that I am a powerful spirit that has taken on the physical experience for the purpose of learning. It has power over me when I am compelled by the wants and impulses and values of my personality. It holds power over me when I fear and hate or when I am in sorrow and fester in anger or when I strike out in rage.

It has no power over me when I love, when compassion opens my heart to others, when my creativity flows joyously into the present moment. Even after my personality becomes conscious and aware of its illusion and sets its intention accordingly, the karmic obligations of my soul must still be met. Karma is karma and energy is energy. I understand this and I try not to respond to the experiences and the events of my life with anger, fear, sorrow or jealousy, which would create additional negative karma for my soul. Now I respond with compassion and trust that the universe in each moment is attending to the needs of my soul. This attracts other souls with the same frequency of consciousness, which means positivity attracts positivity and therefore I must be a loving person so that I can live in a world of loving and positive people.

This is law of attraction. Behind my fears there is powerlessness. I reach outward to fill the places within me that are empty of power, I learn one by one that those places cannot be filled with fear but can be filled with love. It is not worth it to be angry because the parts of my soul that need warmth and companionship for relationships of depth and quality will not be possible for me if I live my life in anger, fear or jealousy. I must know my essential needs and my artificial needs. I must truly distinguish my real needs, what I truly need as a human being and a soul and what I have adopted as artificial needs for reasons based on external power. I must begin to separate myself from my artificial self and choose clearly how I wish to respond and to hold myself accountable when I allow my artificial needs to take over.

Authentic needs belong to my soul, I need to love and to be loved, I need to express my creativity, to cultivate my spirit to work consciously at aligning my personality with my soul. I need to be counseled with the impersonal wisdom of my non-physical teachers and the guidance of my non-physical guides. These are some of my authentic needs, my essential needs for my soul. My artificial needs belong to the personality, they are what I adopt in my physical life in order to maneuver the space I claim and walk in upon the earth.

Artificial needs are the needs from which negative karma is created; it's time to let them go for good. I refuse to be clouded over by my artificial needs because they drain energy from me. My authentic needs will always be met by the universe. The universe supplies me with my authentic needs. I am always being given opportunities to love and be loved but I have always ruined these opportunities because I wanted to satisfy my artificial needs. By responding to my authentic needs and by allowing artificial ones to drop aside as unnecessary defense mechanisms, I will become more open and understanding and compassionate to others. I must learn to address my real needs so that I won't burden myself with behavioral patterns that are not true to my own nature, that cloud me, that give me some artificial persona that I have to live up to.

There is no power in fear or in any of the activities that are generated by fear. To be quite honest I can never truly relax and enjoy life because most of THE time I am worried if I will ever make it. I doubt myself sometimes like everybody else; I live my life in fear sometimes. I wanted external power and I wanted to control my life, I wanted more money in my bank account, I still do, and a bigger house. I wanted an attractive mate, I wanted to impose my way of thinking upon others. These are the standards of my personality, seeking to satisfy its wants but now I must choose differently, I must stand for perfection for the beauty and compassion of each soul. I must stand for the power of love and the clarity of wisdom. I must stand for forgiveness and humbleness.

Power is energy formed by the intentions of my soul, it is the light shaped by the intentions of love and compassion guided by wisdom. When energy leaves me in fear it brings me pain and discomfort. I always experience pain in my stomach, chest or heart, I get so anxious and the anxiety attack is a massive loss of power from my system. Through that energy center my power losses affect the surrounding parts of my body. I lose power when I rage against an injustice, I lose power when I am threatened by others, I lose power when I distance myself from my fellow humans out of resentment or bitterness or a sense of disappointment or unworthiness or superiority. I lose power when

I long for something or someone, when I grieve and when I envy others.

Beneath all of these is a fear that I am vulnerable, that I am not able to cope without the person or the situation that I miss, that I am at a disadvantage without that which I envy. I lose power whenever I fear that is what a loss of power is. It is time for me to release my energies in love and trust. I must be humble and ask for what I really need the universe to provide. I must be free to love and to be who I am and have no artificial standards to live up to. I must seek the joy of giving without reservations. I must forgive, forgive, forgive and not hold others responsible for my experiences. I must stop complaining and expecting too much from others. I lose power when I receive or when I cling to negative experiences that result from decisions I made while I was learning.

I will do all that I can to the fullest of my ability as well as I can and surrender all. I now understand the laws of karma and attraction and their relationship to what I experience. I am able to see the role, of responsible choice and choosing accordingly in each moment. My clarity is the ability to see my soul in action in the physical world. My clarity allows me to experience my fellow humans with compassion instead of my own judgment. My clarity brings forth true compassion, the sharing of passion with others. It allows the energy of my heart to flow. My clarity turns pain into suffering. It sees the dynamic of the personality that is the cause of the pain and the relationship of that dynamic and that experience to the evolution of the soul.

It is my perception in each moment that everything is designed for wholeness and perfection and every aspect serves ultimately a beautiful learning. I try to see the perfection of each situation and each experience for the evolution of my soul and the maturation of each personality involved. I now see perfection in the smallest details everywhere. Whenever I look I see the hand of God. My clarity evaporates my fears and allows me to choose the vertical path and stay on it. It allows me to understand the dynamics of my addiction, what my addictions serve and how they operate and for me to make the choices that will disempower them and empower me. Love is the energy of my soul, love is what heals my personality. There is nothing that cannot be healed by love but love. Humbleness, forgiveness, clarity and love are the dynamics of freedom; they are the foundations of authentic power.

My soul comes to earth with gifts and it does not incarnate only to heal and to balance its energy or to pay its karmic debts but also to contribute its specialness in special ways. I must begin to walk the path that my soul has chosen and that will satisfy my hunger. Authentic empowerment is necessary to accomplish fully the mission of my soul, yet as I move into authentic empowerment I move toward the fulfillment of my soul's agreement with the universe.

I move consciously toward the energy of my soul and I empower myself. I will know my soul's task when the deepest part of me becomes engaged in what I am doing, when my activities and actions become gratifying and purposeful, when what I do serves both myself and others, when I do not tire within but seek the sweet satisfaction of my life and my work that will mean I am doing what I am meant to be doing and experience purposefulness and meaning in my life and in others. I shape most parts of my life with my family and they serve to activate within me an awareness of who I am and what I am here to do in this earth school.

The pains that I suffer, the loneliness that I feel, the experiences that are disappointing or distressing, the addictions and seeming pitfalls of my life, are each doorways to my awareness. Each offers me an opportunity to see beyond the illusion that serves the balancing and growth of my soul. Within each experience of pain or negativity is the opportunity to challenge the perception that lies behind it, the fear that lies behind it and to choose to learn with wisdom. The fear will not vanish immediately but it will disintegrate as I work with courage. When fear will cease to scare me, it cannot stay. When I choose to learn through wisdom, to evolve consciously, my fears surface one at a time in order for me to exorcise them with my inner faith. My guides and teachers continually offer me light; they encourage me in each moment to my fullest growth and development, yet they cannot prevent me from my learning or my growing or moving through my experiences and letting my experiences influence me. This happens even if I am able to communicate with them directly.

My experiences will move me right or left, there is no single optimal path for my soul, there are many optimal paths. With each choice I make I immediately create numerous paths within that choice, one of which is optimal. In other words the optimal path of my soul is the choice of awareness of the vertical path. Once I have made that choice, then come the various forms of enactment. I trust my universe and my non physical guides and teachers to show me my full power and how to use it. I am taking off my restrictions and letting go of what I think is just reward. I trust and create and I am me, the rest is up to my universe and my non physical guides and teachers. My hands were off the steering wheel a long time ago because I realized that I am not the driver in my life and I am not in control at all.

All I know is, "thy will be done", because I trust and have faith in the universe. I have allowed my life to go in to the hands of the universe completely. I am always supported and guided beautifully by my guides and teachers even though I cannot see them or touch them. The guidance happens none the less in its perfection and in its balance. I am now fully aware of it and can put names to non-physical teachers and I have a sense of personal relationship with them and I am loving it. I am not going it alone upon this earth. I am dependent on my guides and teachers. I ask them about anything and we speak about everything. I do what I do for myself and they are always there to assist but they will never do it for me. It is not possible for them to do it for me. I always give them permission to come closer and I ask them to bless me to give me strength and help make responsible decisions in my life.

When I ask for guidance and assistance I simply assume that it is immediately pouring in. I trust the universe that the circumstance that I am in is working toward my best and most appropriate end. There are no "whens" or "ifs" to that, it is, and I release my specifications and say to the universe, "take me where I need to be". I let them go and trust that the universe will provide and so it shall. I let go of all and let my higher self complete its task. I pray, talk and ask a lot to my Divine Intelligence. I am in partnership with my Divine Intelligence and he helps me by strongly guiding me in ways to co-create in the most effective way for my healing and for the fulfillment of my contract.

When I ask for guidance or help I expect to get it. Praying is moving into a personal relationship with Divine Intelligence. It is impossible to have prayer without power. When I pray I draw to me and invoke grace. Grace is uncontaminated conscious light. Prayer brings grace and grace calms me, that is the cycle. Grace is the tranquilizer of my soul and with grace comes a knowing that what I am experiencing is necessary. It calms me, a sense of knowing. I relax into the present moment and I do what I need to do in the present moment. I cannot afford to lose power over the "what ifs" of my life. I keep my power just in the now, in present time. I keep my power just in the day that I am living on earth and not on how to maneuver tomorrow.

I must use all of my worldly connections but not out of panic or fear. I do what I need to do at my end. My choice comes in knowing appropriate timing, clear motivation and trust. I must allow my intuition to guide my timing. I must take it inside, ask how I feel and then move forward. I must allow myself to experience what it is to learn step by step the freedom that comes from being unattached to the outcome but instead operating from an empowered heart. I live in the trust that when it is appropriate, the pieces will fall into place and I will see clearly. Trust allows me to call forth my negativities in order to heal them. It allows me to follow my feelings through my defenses to their sources and to bring them to light. The parts of myself that resist wholeness live in fear. I must be conscious of all that I feel.

I must feel my intentions in my heart and feel what my heart tells me and not what my mind tells me. I will not find God in my intellect because Divine Intelligence is in my heart. I will open myself to my fellow humans more in order to allow myself to experience what I feel toward them and to hear what they feel. My interactions with others form the basis of my growth because I fear what I will find in others. If I allow myself to hear what others have to say, I turn my back on the opportunities that the universe is giving me to find the power of my heart, the power of compassion.

I must have the courage to engage in human relationships so that I can grow. Compassion is mutual. My physical body is soothed and invigorated by the energy of my heart and torn by lower frequency currents of anger, rage, fear and violence. I actually damage my body when I feel or act without compassion. I must be always be in the present energy dynamic by challenging my fears. My fear of growing and of transformation of self is what causes me to want to disengage from the present situation and reach for another. I sometimes feel that I am in a pattern of wanting what I do not have, of seeing the grass on the other side greener. By feeling this I am actually letting energy leak to a future that does not exist.

Each time I feel negative I must stop and acknowledge that I am feeling negative and discharge it consciously, I must go for the root of it in that instant and as I work to pull out the root, simultaneously look at the positive side and remind myself of the greater truth that there is something spiritually profound at work, that my life is no accident, that I am in contact with the universe. Trust allows me to experience a blissful life. I now trust that the universe in each moment is providing for the needs of my soul and that the guidance and assistance of my non-physical guides and teachers is always available to me.

Awakeness is a blissful state, not a painful one. It is blissful; it is fully balanced and lovingly harmonious. It is all of these things and more. The vertical path means clarity, not pain. All I am doing each day is creating what is appropriate and perfect to the evolution of my soul. From now on I will allow myself to become aware of what I feel and give myself permission to choose the most positive behavior in every moment. I am on a journey to find the seat of my soul.

Chapter 15

I am open to people now in ways that I have never been before. I do not need the defenses that I used to have. I am exploring my soul subjects and experiencing the different seasons in my life. I am trying hard to balance the seasons that come and go inside me. I am striving to be conscious of all that I am and to choose responsibly at each moment. I am so relieved that the winter light is over at last and everything is becoming fresh anew, vibrant and wondrous. I found out that it is not only when things are going wrong in my life that I get frightened, it is also when my life is going profoundly right.

My spiritual growth is not an easy escape from the painful circumstances of my life; it's a new beginning to follow my heart and stop being a victim of my circumstance. I must understand that I am a powerful creator in my life. The old is gone and what is emerging is new. I cannot grow spiritually and remain the same. Understanding this is knowledge, seeing it is wisdom and knowing it is trust. As the seasons of my life come and go, I acknowledge the shifts that happen in my life and allow them to mature in their own time.

The different seasons in my life come and go and give way to each other, whether I like it or not. My life is built on this cycle of seasons, on the continual repetition of them. These seasons are given to me for my benefit; they are brought to my awareness so that I can change them. They are avenues to the clarity and love that I am waiting for. The winter light challenged me, confronted me and showed me what I must change in myself. It was a holy and precious season, it illuminated my holy and precious life, it was my potential calling, disguised as a disaster. My new life was staring at me in this winter light. Now I have new and different ways to respond to my tragedies and disasters.

I have active love and it makes me feel warm toward others, appreciative of others and kind. I exchange these currencies of my heart and this is the only way I can bond with other people. I look for what is needed and I provide it. I live directly from my heart without reservation; I realize that what needs to be done is for me to do. I do not restrict my love to my family or those I know or those who look, think, act, dress, and speak like me because if I do that I prevent myself from experiencing the ability to love. Love is unlimited but that does not mean I have to hug and greet everyone I meet, it means my heart can be open to everyone.

I live with an open heart, even while others are frightened. Love is not taking advantage of the vulnerabilities of others. It is making the needs of others as important as my own. Love is the fire that is out of control; I practice moderation in all things except love. I miss my fear and I keep looking around for it, because it was so familiar. There is a huge openness in me now where my fear used to be. Fear became comfortable even though it was painful. The old skin felt natural because I had worn it for a long time. It was my old friend and I finally made the connection between these emotions and the pain in my life and I have changed.

It's a process, I am getting there slowly but surely, I am on a journey of transforming myself into a compassionate, wise man and I am grateful for my life but my fears still call me. When they call me I put them in my window where the light is greatest and appreciate them, then move forward. I am creating authentic power by aligning my personality with my soul and that requires discovering the parts of my personality that are creating destructive consequences and changing them. This new life I have chosen requires me to challenge all my fears and my fears are all I have known for most of my life. They have helped me to navigate though the most difficult times in my life.

I feel naked without them, even though they hurt but the new life that is calling me has no fear in it, which is bliss. I now listen to the wisdom and compassion coming into my consciousness. My fears are no longer important to me, my life is no longer mine alone. I am the compassion of the universe and together we create powerfully. I see the universe as a wise and compassionate partner in my educational process and I am grateful for it. I am becoming more patient because I am taking my time to learn from my experiences. I stop, relax, think and move with the flow in every circumstance that I find myself in and I am aware now. I can see the abundance around me and the value of my experiences.

I built the foundation to support my spiritual growth in order for me to live a new life of kindness and compassion, a life grounded and appropriate in every way. I am aware of my emotions and that requires my full commitment and courage. It is painful to become emotionally aware because there is so much pain in this world and that pain is in me. There is also joy but I cannot reach it until I can reach the pain I feel and only then can I begin to cultivate the sources of my joy and challenge the causes of my pain. Kindness and compassion are the skills I need to develop, awareness of my emotions is my foundation to my spiritual growth.

I now try to share what is true to me with sensitivity because I know sometimes I can be harsh. I am not afraid of confrontations but I love the truth more than I need to be loved. I am exploring some soul questions in my life and soul questions come from a deeper place than other questions in my life. They reach toward meaning and fulfillment. My soul questions come from beyond the intellect and the answers to them reach beyond the intellect. They are doorways though which soul to soul communication enters my life and transform me. How can I love? What is the purpose of my life? How can I change?

I feel such pain? These are my soul questions. I ask these questions because I am longing for a vertical path through life, for transformation, a deeper meaning, fulfillment and love. My soul questions are about changing myself instead of changing others, THEY are part of my pursuit of authentic power and wholeness. All the answers that nurture me come from the universe and I recognize them by my resonance. when I hear, read or have an intuition about them, then it is for me to decide whether or not to pay attention to them, to apply them in my life and see what they produce. So far they have made me humbler, clearer, more forgiving and more loving and I will continue to apply them and experiment with them. These soul questions inspire me to ask more soul questions and to open myself to the answers, that is the purpose of my soul questions; to deepen my experiences and open myself to them again and again until all that is left is the power and beauty of the life I am creating and giving to others.

How do I know? What is my philosophy based on? How do I know that what I have written is only an illusion, a fantasy or whether it has value? These are questions I ask myself. I know what I know because I now pay attention to my experiences. I listen to my inner sense of what is worth listening to, I get attracted to certain things or maybe they attract me. When I feel it I make a point of remembering what I have heard and applying, it to see if it works for me. Something just happens within me, it's like the words are talking to me and it makes me want to find out more about the source of other people's insights. I look inside myself, trust what I have recognized and make them my own insights.

I am using my life as an experiment with truth. The minute I hear something that I recognize as true for me, I try it out. If it works I incorporate it into my life and use it. If I recognize something I read or see on TV or hear on the radio as true for me, that recognition makes it my own truth. My ideas and insights come from the universe. They are not mine. The universe is the source and I am the recipient. I am the authority in my life and I use my authority to accept what I recognize as true for me. I am learning to draw upon myself for the answers that I need in my life, not because the old people are gone but because what worked in the past no longer works today. Old ways now lead only to painful consequences.

I value what I hear and see from my heart, my guides and teachers, my God, my Divine Intelligence, my universe and the world around me. What I say, what I choose and what I shape my personality to be with my choices is important. Everything in this earth school is important. The universe is alive, wise and compassionate. No thought is unheard and no prayer goes unanswered although not always in the way that I expect. My universe did not burden me with a destiny, it provided me with lots of potential and how much of that potential I realize depends on the choices that I make moment by moment. There is always wisdom in my choices because each of them create consequences that I will experience. I must choose to learn from them.

My thoughts open me or close me. The thought that I might not be able to get out of my financial debts closes me; the thought that the universe is my friend opens me. What my thoughts open or close me to is my experience, they determine whether I will fear and resist my experiences or whether I will embrace them and be supported by them. I am a spiritual person now because I am more aware of my emotions, consciousness and intentions and I am taking responsibility for all my choices. I am grateful to be alive every day, even during difficult experiences. My life is filled with meaning and purpose and my creativity is unlimited. I enjoy myself more these days. I am fulfilled, I treasure life in all its forms. I was born to be a spiritual person and every day I am working to change and create a more compassionate self and world

I became aware of my fears such as anger, disappointment jealousy. I thought I was aware of all of them but I had to look deeper because beneath that anger there was a lot of emotional pain. It was easier for me to become angry with someone else or myself or even God than to feel the pain. That pain was a direct, unfiltered experience of fear. By simply recognizing when I was angry was not enough, I had to go to the root of the emotion, which is part of my personality that I do not know about or am too afraid or ashamed of to acknowledge. I challenged this experience and I no longer want it in my energy system.

Challenging this part of my personality was a decision to use my free will to change an aspect of myself that I did not want, creating experiences in my life anymore. I realized if I do not challenge my fears I would die with them because growing older does not mean that automatically I will become gentler or wiser. No one can change me except myself. I challenge the frightened parts of my personality by choosing not to behave as I normally have in the past, when these parts of my personality become active. When I feel impatient I can now choose to stop and consider the other person's needs, instead of my own. When I feel the need to say "yes" in order to please I can say "no" instead because I am now true to myself.

I do it my way, recognizing and challenging frightened parts of my personality that I want to change and recognizing and cultivating loving parts of my personality that I want to strengthen for my spiritual growth. I am fully conscious of everything I am feeling all the time but it is difficult to become emotionally aware because many of my emotions are painful. My painful emotions offer me the opportunity I need to grow spiritually because they originate in the frightened parts of my personality that I need to locate, challenge and heal in order to grow to my full potential.

I am developing spiritually because eventually I saw that everything is sacred and every form of life is sacred. The universe is sacred, I am sacred and all that I do is sacred, so whenever I take time to know myself or to appreciate my life and the lives of others, I open myself to the experiences of sacred life. I do the same thing when I pray or write my thoughts in my journal. Coming to see everything as sacred everywhere is what I see as my spiritual development. My destiny was not written for me; I was born with lots of potential, not limited destiny. Whether or not I reach the fullest potential that is available to me is a matter of the choices I make.

At this point I am leaving the life path that I am now on and embarking on one that is more compassionate, wise, fulfilling and free. Not even my non-physical teachers know what I will choose in my tomorrow. I try not to squander my moments exploring the "what ifs" of my life because they are endless and unlimited. My external experiences reflect my internal experiences. What is behind my eyes is more important than what is in front of them. I cannot change the reflection in the mirror without changing what the mirror reflects and that requires inner work on myself. This is

146

how I change what the mirror reflects. Every individual I have encountered or will encounter is my soul-mate. My challenge is to determine how I will relate with the millions of soul-mates I will encounter in the course of my lifetime.

The relationships I have now are with fellow souls and I now understand that my past relationships illuminated parts of my personality that were unhealed, such as the parts that dominate others, please others, judge others and exploit them. Changing my relationships will not heal those parts of myself and new relationships will continue to illuminate the same unhealed parts in me until I heal them. I must find and heal the frightened parts of my personality that created these issues so that I won't recreate them in my next relationship. I must be patient and start thinking about other people's needs, I should not expect anything from anybody. My soul-mates are not my saviors, they are students like me in this earth school. I must forgive more because it is not possible for someone to take advantage of my forgiveness.

Forgiveness does not have anything to do with me. Forgiveness is letting go of my resentment, disappointment, anger and hurt. When I do I become free from these prisons, they no longer captivate my attention, I am no longer steeped in anger and righteous indignation, I no longer feel the need to convince others that I have been wronged. I give up being a victim and step into a lighter, less restricted consciousness. Forgiveness is self-healing; not forgiving is holding on to my expectations and forgiving is realizing them. Many people have betrayed me because I had expectations about them that they did not fulfill. I have learned that forgiving means letting go of those expectations. It's hard but if I do that, no one can betray me and there is no way that I can feel betrayed or hurt.

Forgiveness allows me to see clearly instead of through the filters of my desires. Once I see clearly I act appropriately and if that requires that I change my relationships, I can do that with an open heart. I do not have to resent someone in order to make a change in my life. I can only do it because it is appropriate because I see changes that I want to make and I make them. Forgiving is choosing a light and joyful heart instead of anger and resentment. I must love without fear or expectation and it is actually a good thing to be in a relationship with someone who stimulates my fears because spiritual partnership is a partnership between equals for the purpose of spiritual growth. All my love relationships helped me grow spiritually. My fears show me what I need to work on.

They are what needs to be changed and healed in myself. I have a lot of issues with my personality, which means I have got a lot of inner work to do in myself. I have always wanted to fall in love but now I know that love is not something I fall into, love must be cultivated and developed and it requires my patience and dedication. I must have the ability to care about others. Love is not a sentimental feeling, it is experiencing my deep connection with all of life. It is my ability to feel the pain of others. I am no longer concerned about falling in love but I want my life to be filled with love. I always judge people which is seeing myself as superior, wiser, smarter or as Mr Know-It-All to other people.

When I judge I create painful consequences for myself. I always judge the experiences or situations that I find myself in and say, why me? This is so unfair. Judgment is accompanied by negative emotional reactions. It is when I don't like what I see and when I resist what I experience. It is when I want a situation or person to be different and when I have expectations that are not satisfied. When that happens I lose energy and power. I must start seeing a person or a circumstance as it is, which is discerning. Judgment has an emotional charge to it, it makes one person a victim and another a villain. Discernment allows me to observe, analyze with my heart and act accordingly.

I get so irritated by some people and just cannot handle them sometimes, even if I try to avoid them. I found out those people that irritate me were mirroring the reflection of myself because when I do not want to see something about myself I become irritated when I see it in others. I was actually projecting, I intensely dislike in others what I do not want to recognize in myself. I now pay attention when I am irritated because that will be my clue that there is something that I can learn about myself from an interaction with another person this is my emotional reaction to the interaction.

I always found myself on yo-yo diets and sometimes I even starved myself trying to maintain my weight. It was a mission to maintain it because I kept going back to my old habits. The thing I did not consider when I thought of a healthy diet was my thoughts. My thoughts were toxins because I wanted to be lean and mean for competition and to be loved by others and to fit in and be popular. I did all my diets for the wrong reasons. I was not content with myself, I needed approval and those thoughts were toxins to my body, sabotaging my healthy diet. Now I treat myself kindly, no longer obsessed about my weight. I take time and listen to what my body wants and that showed me the addictions I have to work on and also showed me what gives me energy and strength. I now do what I can to maintain a vital and healthy body. My job is to develop the ability to listen and not follow my compulsions or the unexamined advice of others. My body will always tell me what it needs if I listen carefully.

Chapter 16

When I dream I dream in vivid colors but one thing is for sure, when I wake up I sometimes cannot remember the whole dream, which used to stress me. I found out later in my life that all those dreams I could not remember where just unimportant information, which my brain was getting rid of. The dreams I remember are comments on my life, they are valuable perspectives on my life that are meant to inform me of what I need to consider at that moment. My dreams are my nightly letters, they are messages from my soul, they are meant to tell me something that is important for me to know about myself at that moment in my life. Each dream I dream about myself brings me new messages, the latest breaking news available in special editions prepared just for my viewing. How I use these special edition communications from my soul is really up to me.

I have habits and some of them I do because I do not want to feel anxious or uncomfortable emotions, feelings of a workaholic and perfectionism. I also have addictions and most of those I do because I feel an irresistible urge to do them. There is an overpowering feeling of irresistible attraction to them and I end up engaging in my addictions. I do this to avoid my painful emotions. My addictions are my greatest inadequacies, they are parts of myself that are out of control. I can choose to leave them out of my control or do something about them. The healing of my addictions is the beginning of my story, not the end of it. I must make a choice because I need to be healthy and actually I do not need a reason for my addictive experiences; their power is strong but I will challenge them. The more I challenge them the more they will lose power over me; eventually their power over me will disintegrate. Healing my obsessions, compulsions and addictions is the work that I was born to do because they stand between me and the life that my soul desires. I cannot create what my soul wants to create while I am obsessed, compelled or addicted. The process of finding the unhealed parts of myself does not last forever. I celebrate that I am on the path at last toward wholeness.

I am aware of my painful emotions and now recognize how my body feels and the types of thoughts that I have when they are present. I will no longer label them as anger, fear, doubt or anything else, I will know them as old familiar experiences that I want to change. I choose to be grateful and optimistic. I now cultivate and grow, I know it will take time and effort but I have got vision and perseverance. I am aware of some of the parts of my personality that need healing. My awareness has increased and also the number of opportunities I have to challenge them have increased. I used to get so livid when things did not go the way I expected them to, but now I am more open to change.

I love my life, I embrace my experiences, no matter how difficult or pleasing. And I trust that they are perfect for me to grow. I have no fear, I trust the universe completely. I have some bad memories and painful experiences and now I can finally heal them by knowing what cannot be changed and changing what can be changed. I compare what I created then with what I want to create now and use my experiences to help me create differently. I am grateful that I will no longer create again what I created in the past.

I always felt the need to compete with others because I feared that I would not be able to take care of myself. I feared that I was not lovable; I feared that my life was meaningless. I wanted to shine and prove to everyone that I was the best. I made stupid decisions which were lessons, putting myself in debt because I wanted to buy things I could not afford. I so wanted to fit in and be the talk of the town, only to find out that there is nothing to compete for or anyone to compete with. It was just so unnecessary because I am a creative, and powerful, compassionate and loving spirit.

So are my fellow students in this earth school. The universe provides me with what my soul needs and not what my personality desires. I have always wondered why my relationships do not last long; it was my behaviors, attitude and my expectations. These might have contributed to the end of my relationships. I was always attempting to please at the beginning, showing them my good side and when that phase ended, I would try to dominate them or control them in some other way. I would be competitive and judgmental and eventually I would lose interest and start to be unfaithful. These are the parts I played in my past relationships.

My expectations were a burden on my relationships. I wanted things to go my way and I was not willing to compromise or even apologize when I was in the wrong. I was always right and I wanted to change them. I am so glad that I am learning more about myself from my experiences than I can from other people and I can change myself with what I am learning about myself but I cannot change other people, that is for them to do.

I have forgiven myself for all the bad decisions I made and I feel lighter now because I have left all my baggage behind. My protective walls are tumbling down, the fear and uncertainty is gone. I am learning to trust and have faith in all the affairs that I have with my soul-mates. I have decided to change myself and do things differently. I make responsible choices, I am experimenting with my life and that change has already begun. I know that I have a choice and that what I experience is what I am choosing to experience. I am intending to create harmony, cooperation, sharing and contributing to others, that's me from now on.

I am changing to be an authentic empowered being. I feel so alive and I am grateful to my God that he decided to create me, to give me gifts that I was born to give and nothing is going to keep me from doing that. That is my purpose here on earth school. I am filled with enthusiasm, joy and gratitude that I can to take this journey of aligning my soul with my personality. It is so exciting; the more authentic power I develop, the more freedom I will have to experiment with my life and the more desire I will have to experiment with. As I become authentically powerful I am drawn naturally to activities that are more meaningful to me and those are activities what my soul wants to do. I am beginning to see that all of my experiences even those of despair, of having no reason for living and of being alone, they all have a purpose. My experiences of being unfulfilled and lonely are powerful but I have the power and will to change them. I am worthy of my life and I intend to live it accordingly.

My life now is my meditation. I try to balance it and find my center by observing my emotions in terms of the physical sensations in my body, especially my solar plexus, chest and throat area. I challenge painful parts of myself that need healing and when they are active I hurt. I cultivate the loving and nurturing parts of myself and when they are active my physical sensations are pleasing. I also pay close attention when I speak or act and if I forget I pay attention to them again when I remember.

My intention is the reason or motivation for acting and it is also what creates the consequences I will encounter. I am more open to what my experiences tell me about myself rather than what they might tell me about other people. I especially notice what I do not like about people because I know that my reactions to other people show me parts of my personality that I am not aware of or that I have been avoiding to healing. I also try to enjoy myself and the perfection of the moment. As they say, if you know how to worry you know how to meditate. Everything I do every day part of my meditation. I worry about creating bad karma for myself so I watch every move and action and every negative thought in my head. I am more at peace with myself and I am finding and dealing with parts of myself that I have been avoiding for many years. I am happier and lighter because I do not have doubt or fear in my life. All I have is trust and faith in the universe. Thy will shall be done. Lastly I try to make responsible choices and decisions in my life. It's all about choices, moment by moment.

The real world is a world of compassion and wisdom. It is a living universe that supports my spiritual growth in every way. The brutality, suffering and violence in our world IS there because we created them and the remedy to all this chaos is not to withdraw from what we have created but to create differently and responsibly.

Chapter 17

I am becoming happier by focusing on daily behaviors, my state of mind and my consciousness because these are the most immediately changeable factors that have the greatest impact on my happiness. They hold the key to changing my life circumstances in a positive way. The truth is that my happiness is determined more by my state of mind than by the external circumstances of my life. The happiness in my life depends on the quality of the thoughts in my head, not the quantity of dollars in my pocket. I was not happy and I changed my attitude and now I only do what makes me happy because I know that my happiness is an inside job.

I confused success with happiness and I tried to buy happiness with success; I thought success and happiness were the same thing but happiness is more than success. I believed that my happiness depends on being successful, that unhappiness could be avoided by being successful. So the unhappier I was about my previous situation, the more I pursued my success and tried to prove to myself that this strategy was working. I also wanted pleasure, which for short periods of time at least felt like happiness, but because happiness equals pleasure and meaning, my unhappiness only grew. I chased the false goals of success and pleasure above anything else and hoped that it would eventually bring me happiness.

Happiness based on success is a moving target. I realize that I will always have unfulfilled or unsatisfied desires because desires can never be satisfied once and for all. For every desire satisfied another is created. It's the revolving door of desire, one after the next it, never ends. I have learned to accept that I will always be incomplete when it comes to my desires.

I took the decision to make happiness my top priority. I stopped letting other people tell me what I wanted, I became independent of the opinions of others and I stopped searching for approval and acceptance from others. I am spending my life in my own way and I have learned to tell the difference between what comes from within and what is imposed on me from outside. I acted as though comfort and luxury were the chief requirements of my life when all I needed to make me happy was something to be enthusiastic about. I gave up trying to make success my path to happiness and I decided to make happiness my main goal and by doing this I am more likely to be successful because happiness comes before and leads to success.

For happiness I do not need to have the right friends and the right connections or get the right education, live in a mansion house, look the right way or age, work in the right industry or make more money. I simply have to do what I can with what I have from where I am. I am doing things differently now because if I do not put my happiness first I will keep getting the same results, which is unhappiness in my life. I spend more time with love ones, take time for myself even if that means losing lots of money, exercise more, eat better, sleep more and spend more time outdoors. I have a career I love, which is the good fit for my personality and strength. I use cash instead of credit, buy basic functional appliances, furniture and cars.

I gave up my single-minded pursuit of success and I chose to grow authentic happiness instead and it is cheaper and better for me. my mantra these days is when it comes to happiness, the right way is often the easy way, so I live my life by working smart, not hard because when I am working hard that means I am doing something wrong. What I do now is work hard at the right things and it's actually easy because it does not feel like hard work at all. I try to put more energy into things that make me happy. I invest my time and energy wisely in things that bring me the most fulfillment and satisfaction and when I do, life flows effortlessly. It feels like I am taking the path of least resistance. My happiness involves both pleasure and meaning I think I am a provider and it makes me happy when I make or provide for my loved ones. I think the day I bought a house for my family, a shelter, a place where they can call home was the happiest. I was enthusiastic and excited. Those kind and giving activities brought the most natural effortless and feeling of great happiness.

These themes are my happiness islands. I am good at organizing and that makes me think of all the successful parties I have organized. The one that made me happier was my sister's 21st birthday. I was happy that day, I even cried tears of joy. I was surprised at myself, asking how I pulled it off. Another event was when I did three unveilings of tombstones for my family. I wanted to do it and it was effortless and natural to me. Organizing is my natural strength and doing things in which I can apply my strength gives me a sense of meaning and purpose. These themes are my achievement islands.

I spend my time trying to get the most happiness "bang" for my "energy buck". I look for those things that give me the biggest reward happiness-wise, for the least amount of effort. I try to balance every activity by staying attuned to how I feel as I spend time in my activities. As long as I feel inspired, strong and energized I keep going but as soon as I feel drained, tired, weak and uninspired I stop at "good enough". I am getting better and better at identifying exactly when I have maximized my happiness profit within a certain activity.

I go with the flow of life and surround myself with happy people. I have learned to let the present be what it is, a gift in its own right because true joy comes from being fully present in each and every moment, not just when things are going my way. I appreciate what I have and who I am and I refuse to be dependent on other people to supply me with what I need to be happy. I do not limit my happiness by giving it conditions and I try to remember that when I feel negative emotion it is a sign that I am comparing what is to what I think should be or could be. I am in the present moment without judgment or expectations and be happy.

I am the master of the weather in my own skies and I do not make my happiness dependent on other people's behavior. I get high off my own supply and I make my happiness dependent on me and only me. I have learned to want what I have and get what I want. The universe gives me more of what I am grateful for. I try to focus on what feels good and this takes a lot of practice.

I have learned to change the topic, station or scenery when things are not going well. I feed the good seeds in my life with attention and starve the bad seeds with indifference. I practice non-resistance because I know now that what I fight I invite. I do not try to stop a thought; I just observe it and question it or replace it with a more empowering one. I do not try to solve problems when I am feeling bad, I wait until I am feeling better. I measure myself by my best moments, not my worst. I appreciate what I have and who I am without asking for things to be different.

I have learned to accept what I cannot change. I stopped comparing myself to others and I ignore what others have and have accomplished. I am now more selective as to what I watch on TV, read and listen to. I have made my happiness dependent on me and only me because I control myself beautifully, effortlessly and successfully, thought by thought. I am free of all addictions to people and things. I am addicted only to feeling good and the only person who can make me feel good is me. I love myself and I love my independence and I am living every moment of my life. I am realizing more and more that I am and have always been self-sufficient and independent.

I am a strong, loving, independent, freedom seeking man. I love myself and that love is independent of what everybody else says or thinks. I am becoming more confident and comfortable in my own skin. My thoughts and opinions are louder and clearer than the thoughts of everyone else out there and that means mastering my life, one thought at a time. I unconditionally love myself inside and out and nothing can change that. I am God's gift to myself and God is perfect because I am his creation. I am perfect, I am everything I have ever needed or wanted. I have made myself my top priority. I choose my language carefully and edit my speech according to how it makes me feel. I reach for a positive feeling before I speak. I make my vocabulary more positive by using optimistic words and language.

I have realized that there is no such thing as failure, only feedback on the mistakes I have made in the past and this has provided me with opportunities to get clearer about who I am and what I can be. Every experience is a blessing, nothing more and nothing less. My troubles revealed my hidden strength and they helped me identify my real friends because when times got tough I found out who was really there for me. My troubles allowed me to slow down and reevaluate what is most important in my life. It brought things into sharp contrast, which helped me choose the right friends and the happiest path.

I experienced how it was not to really know who I am and have made peace with where I am. I can make different, more loving, more joyous, more evolved choices about who I will become. My life will never be perfect because I will never be perfect, I will always be facing new challenges in my life. I can never get to a place where I am immune from difficulty or misfortune. Now I see the value of diversity and I notice the strengths adversity reveals. I recognize and appreciate the relationships that are left behind and the ones that remain and are strengthened. I choose happy over realistic. I do not let adversity undermine my optimism about my future, even if having low expectations seems logical.

I have complete control over my mood all day every day. I always have the freedom to choose what I focus on and what I think, which is happiness. I reach for better thoughts before I act, which means I take the emotional journey first then take the action journey when it is inspired and unfolds naturally from a place of inspiration and joy. I do the inside out approach (feel-have-do). I pursue intrinsic goals, goals that are rewarding in and of themselves, goals that satisfy my inherent psychological needs, such as the need to be helpful to others. Happiness is the way. I put myself and my happiness first and make my own rules as I go. I stay liquid, stay loose, I am formless. I use what works for me and lose what does not. Most of all I just keep learning in the direction of what feels good, the rest will take care of itself.

The relationship I have with myself is the most important one. Finding myself, picking my brain, controlling my thoughts, finding God, making friends with myself and God and knowing that I will never be alone and was never alone. I began a love affair that will last a lifetime. I treat myself the way I want others to treat me, teaching them how to treat me. Self love is a pre-requisite for loving others. The happiness, love and appreciation I seek does not exist out there in the world, it is hiding inside me.

When I am happy first and make nothing more important than feeling good, the right relationship for me will develop. When the right relationship does develop I will find myself more easily overcoming my stumbling blocks, the insecurities, power dynamics, games and other issues that turned my relationships into stones and ruined opportunities to express greater love, appreciation and freedom. There is only one kind of love and that is unconditional love. Hoping or wanting somebody to be different or better in any way so that I can be happy puts me in a helpless state of mind and a powerless state of being. I have learned to love others unconditionally. I look for and find the best in them and leave the other stuff out of the picture. I have accepted and love everybody for who and what they are without asking them to be different. I remember every time that I do not get to make the decision to change the other person's behavior because that is their decision and my happiness depends on my thoughts, words and actions and those are decisions or choices I always have complete control over.

The relationship I have with myself sets the tone for all other relationships in my life. The only person who can fulfill, satisfy, impress, delight, inspire or empower me is me. What others say or do has nothing to do with me and I cannot make everybody happy, that is a fact. I am conscious enough to know that authentic happiness comes from inside. I remember that words do not teach, only experience teaches. I am the example of what I teach. I focus on what makes me feel good and when I do that my entire life and those of the people around me will turn in the direction of those thoughts, shifting from negative to positive like a tide.

By building on my unique strength and helping others to build on their unique strengths I can learn and teach others how to spend more time in flow, joy and happiness. I exploit what is already working, look for, focus on, think about and talk about what I appreciate and the best of what exists in my life and the lives of those people around me. I made peace with where I am by finding things to appreciate right here, right now.

I am more present and have made peace with the present by finding things in my life and reality to appreciate now. I do not rush into things, out of things or through things any more. I take my time and savor things more. I put all my energy, attention and intention into finding that which brings me meaning and pleasure. I am persistent and I am getting better at all of this only by practicing. I know if I recruit and practice thoughts, words and actions that feel good I will always experience happiness and I will always attract good things.

Everything I want or need is available to me; all I have to do is practice appreciative thoughts, words and actions. There is nothing I cannot be or do or have in this world. Faith is in me and I believe in God. I know and trust that the better I feel, the greater the chances that better things are on their way to me. I enhance and exaggerate those positive feelings by looking for evidence and proof that things are working out. I remember that sometimes good things are usually long on their way to me before I can see any proof of it. Good things come to those who wait that is why I have learned to be patient and persevere because God's timing is perfect every time. I learned this the hard way believe me I know.

The promotion is mine long before I get the appointment letter, my new spiritual partner is on the way as I write this, the money I want is on its way to me long before I actually see it in my cheque account. I am an Investec elite client and that is a fact. I love the picture of my zebra on my charge card. The truth is, there is no better time to be happy than right now. My life will always be filled with challenges. The best thing for me is to admit this and decide to be happy anyway. I treasure every moment I have and treasure it even more because I am making the decision to do so, time waits for no one. I stopped waiting because happiness is here now, waiting inside me waiting to be seized and used. I just need to tap into my happiness now!

I appreciate the effort that I am making trying to make myself happy. I appreciate my effort in trying to align my personality with my soul and finding the seat to my soul. I appreciate my effort in trying to be more intimate with my God and finding the purpose for my life, discovering my shape in order to use it to help others and serve my God. I appreciate the effort I am making to change myself to be Christ-like and defeating my demons, I appreciate the fact that God is always giving me a fresh start to make things better. I am wiser now and I always have the support I need from my guides and teachers. I believe and trust and I have faith that thy will be done. I appreciate the fact that I am more in touch with myself and I am making an effort to know myself more, besides my flaws and weaknesses. I took the first step in courage to discover myself and my intuitive voice and to trust my gut feeling more. I am more comfortable and content in my own skin. I am what I am. I am my own special creation and I have accepted that and I am moving on into great discoveries. I am taking this journey moment by moment. End of my story.